THE STATE CHILDREN'S HEALTH INSURANCE PROGRAM (SCHIP):
ISSUES AND ANALYSES

THE STATE CHILDREN'S HEALTH INSURANCE PROGRAM (SCHIP):
ISSUES AND ANALYSES

ARTHUR B. ROSE
EDITOR

Novinka Books
New York

Senior Editors: Susan Boriotti and Donna Dennis
Coordinating Editor: Tatiana Shohov
Office Manager: Annette Hellinger
Graphics: Wanda Serrano and Matt Dallow
Editorial Production: Maya Columbus, Alexis Klestov, Vladimir Klestov,
   Matthew Kozlowski and Lorna Loperfido
Circulation: Ave Maria Gonzalez, Vera Popovic, Luis Aviles, Sean Corkery,
   Raymond Davis, Melissa Diaz, Meagan Flaherty, Magdalena Nuñez,
   Marlene Nuñez, Jeannie Pappas and Frankie Punger
Communications and Acquisitions: Serge P. Shohov
Marketing: Cathy DeGregory

Library of Congress Cataloging-in-Publication Data

The state children's health insurance program (SCHIP): issues and analyses / Arthur B. Rose (editor).
   p. cm.
Includes index
ISBN 1-59033-903-7 (softcover)
1. Child health services—Finance. 2. Insurance, Health. 3. Children—Medical care. 4. Medicaid. [DNLM: 1. State Children's Health Insurance Program (U.S.) 2. Insurance, Health—economics—Child—United States. 3. Insurance, Health—legislation & jurisprudence—Child—United States. 4. Child Health Services—United States. 5. Medicaid—Child—United States. 6. State Government—United States. W 250 AA1 S7968 2003] I. Rose, Arthur B.

RJ102.S735 2003
362.198'92'000973—dc22   2003028109

Copyright © 2004 by Novinka Books, an imprint of
   Nova Science Publishers, Inc.
   400 Oser Ave, Suite 1600
   Hauppauge, New York 11788-3619
   Tele. 631-231-7269   Fax 631-231-8175
   e-mail: Novascience@earthlink.net
   Web Site: http://www.novapublishers.com

All rights reserved. No part of this book may be reproduced, stored in a retrieval system or transmitted in any form or by any means: electronic, electrostatic, magnetic, tape, mechanical photocopying, recording or otherwise without permission from the publishers.

The publisher has taken reasonable care in the preparation of this book, but makes no expressed or implied warranty of any kind and assumes no responsibility for any errors or omissions. No liability is assumed for incidental or consequential damages in connection with or arising out of information contained in this book. Any parts of this book based on government reports are so indicated and copyright is claimed for those parts to the extent applicable to compilations of such works.

This publication is designed to provide accurate and authoritative information with regard to the subject matter covered herein. It is sold with the clear understanding that the publisher is not engaged in rendering legal or any other professional services. If legal or any other expert assistance is required, the services of a competent person should be sought. FROM A DECLARATION OF PARTICIPANTS JOINTLY ADOPTED BY A COMMITTEE OF THE AMERICAN BAR ASSOCIATION AND A COMMITTEE OF PUBLISHERS.

Printed in the United States of America

CONTENTS

Foreword		**vii**
Chapter 1	SCHIP Financing Issues *Evelyne Parizek Baumrucker and Peter Kraut*	**1**
Chapter 2	Medicare Provisions in the Medicare, Medicaid, and SCHIP Benefits Improvement and Protection Act of 2000 (BIPA, P.L. 106-554) *Hinda Ripps Chaikind, Sibyl Tilson, Jennifer O'Sullivan, Carolyn Merck and Madeleine Smith*	**43**
Chapter 3	Reaching Low-Income, Uninsured Children: Are Medicaid and SCHIP doing the Job? *Elicia Herz and Evelyne Parizek Baumrucker*	**87**
Chapter 4	State Children's Health Insurance Program: A Brief Overview *Elicia J. Herz and Peter Kraut*	**121**
Chapter 5	The State Children's Health Insurance Program: Eligibility, Enrollment, and Program Funding *Evelyne P. Baumrucker*	**139**
Index		**171**

FOREWORD

The State Children's Health Insurance Program (SCHIP) offers federal matching funds for states and territories to provide health insurance to uninsured, low-income children in families whose annual incomes are too high to qualify for Medicaid. Unlike Medicaid, which operates as an individual entitlement, SCHIP operates as a capped grant program. Allotment of funds among states is determined by a formula set in law. Once a state depletes a given year's original allotment, other than funds from prior years made available through redistribution, no additional federal funds will be made available to that state for that year. States have the flexibility to design their programs to operate within these funding constraints. The allotment and redistribution methods under current law have been incompatible with state spending patterns to date. This book details the issues necessary to understand and track this important program.

SCHIP financing issues are being addressed by the 108th Congress because states with unspent funds from the FY1998 and FY1999 reallocations are interested in recouping those expired amounts and want to make sure that other unspent amounts from subsequent years remain available to their programs. Chapter one discusses these issues.

Chapter two discusses the Medicare, Medicaid, and SCHIP Benefits Improvement and Protection Act of 2000 (BIPA, P.L. 106-554) which included provisions that were designed to increase payments for many of the services covered by the Medicare program, such as hospitals, Medicare+Choice organizations, home health agencies, and skilled nursing facilities. The legislation also included limited expansions of certain preventive benefits and modifies the appeals and coverage processes.

Chapter three provides general background information on the current status of eligibility, enrollment, and outreach issues for children under

Medicaid and SCHIP. It analyzes recent enrollment statistics and factors contributing to those trends. Several issues concerning enrollment facilitation and outreach strategies are also discussed.

Chapter four provides an overview of the key features of the State Children's Health Insurance Program (SCHIP). The key features addressed include eligibility, benefits, cost-sharing, financing, legislative history, and current enrollment and expenditure data.

SCHIP represents the largest publicly funded effort to provide health insurance to children since the enactment of Medicaid in 1965. The program offers federal matching funds for states and territories to provide health insurance coverage to uninsured, low-income children from families whose annual incomes are higher than Medicaid eligibility thresholds. Chapter five discusses this issue.

Chapter 1

SCHIP FINANCING ISSUES[*]

Evelyne P. Baumrucker and Peter Kraut

INTRODUCTION

The State Children's Health Insurance Program (SCHIP) offers federal matching funds for states and territories to provide health insurance to uninsured, low-income children in families whose annual incomes are too high to qualify for Medicaid. Unlike Medicaid, which operates as an individual entitlement, SCHIP operates as a capped grant program. Allotment of funds among states is determined by a formula set in law. Once a state depletes a given year's original allotment, other than funds from prior years made available through redistribution, no additional federal funds will be made available to that state for that year. States have the flexibility to design their programs to operate within these funding constraints.

The allotment and redistribution methods under current law have been incompatible with state spending patterns to date. Spending in the first several years of the program was well below appropriations — cumulative expenditure data through the end of FY2002 show that states spent approximately 46.9% of all federal funds available since the start of the program. Relative to state spending, the appropriation levels were high early on as it took time for states to set up their programs and build enrollment.

---

[*] Excerpted from CRS Report RL31977. Updated August 15, 2003.

Once programs are established, states differ in the extent to which they utilize their allotment.

FY2002 is the first fiscal year in which total spending exceeded that year's appropriations. This trend is likely to continue as additional states spend all of their available funds and are eligible for redistributions. Further, FY2002 is the first of 3 years in which the total federal appropriation is 26% less than it was for each of FY1998-FY2001. At the end of FY2002 $1.3 billion of the FY1998 and FY1999 reallocations expired from the program and CBO predicts an additional $1.4 billion to expire at the close of FY2003. While more states will be eligible for redistributions, there will be fewer funds available for redistribution to such states. In fact, the Centers for Medicare and Medicaid Services (CMS) projects shortfalls for some states over the second half of the program, (FY2003-FY2006).

SCHIP financing issues are being addressed by the 108th Congress because states with unspent funds from the FY1998 and FY1999 reallocations are interested in recouping those expired amounts and all states want to make sure that other unspent amounts from subsequent years remain available to their programs. On June 26, 2003, the Senate passed legislation, S. 312, which would extend the availability of expired funds and establish a new method for redistributing unspent FY2000 and FY2001 allotments among all states. For specified years, S. 312 would also allow "qualifying states" to use up to 20% of their available SCHIP funds for certain Medicaid medical assistance payments. The House-passed bill, H.R. 531, is identical to S. 312 except that it does not include the latter provision. On July 25, 2003, the House passed a new version of the bill, H.R. 2854, to restore unspent SCHIP funds to all states according to the method described in S. 312. H.R. 2854 also establishes alternative criteria for states that would qualify to use up to 20% of their available SCHIP funds for certain Medicaid medical assistance payments. On July 31, 2003 the Senate passed H.R. 2854; the bill was signed into law on August 15, 2003 as P.L. 108-74. This report will be updated as legislative activity occurs.

BACKGROUND

The State Children's Health Insurance Program (SCHIP), created under the Balanced Budget Act of 1997, is the largest publicly funded effort to provide health insurance to children since Medicaid was enacted in 1965. The program offers capped allotments of federal matching funds for states and territories to provide health insurance to uninsured, low-income children in families whose annual incomes are too high to qualify for Medicaid.

Unlike Medicaid which operates as an individual entitlement, SCHIP operates as a capped grant program to the states.[1] States have the flexibility to design their SCHIP programs to operate within the program's funding constraints. States may choose from three options when designing their SCHIP programs. They may expand Medicaid, create a new "separate state" insurance program, or devise a combination of both approaches.[2] Within broad federal guidelines, each state can define the group of targeted low-income children who may enroll in SCHIP.[3] In addition, states can apply to waive program requirements to cover other groups.

Schip Program Financing

The original enactment appropriated federal matching grants totaling $39.7 billion for SCHIP for FY1998 through FY2007. The Department of Health and Human Services (DHHS) and the Centers for Medicare and Medicaid Services (CMS), as the administering agencies for SCHIP, have no discretion over SCHIP spending levels and initial annual allocations of funds

---

[1] Medicaid, authorized under Title XIX of the Social Security Act, is a joint federal state entitlement program that pays for Medicaid assistance primarily for low-income persons who are aged, blind, disabled, members of families with dependent children as well as certain other pregnant women and children. States are required to provide Medicaid benefits to all individuals who meet the state-specific eligibility criteria and apply. As an openended entitlement there are no limits on the federal payments for Medicaid; however, the state must contribute its share of the matching funds in order to continue receiving federal payments.

[2] Services for targeted low-income children who are enrolled in Medicaid are paid from SCHIP allotments at the enhanced matching rate. If SCHIP funds are no longer available, services for these children are paid for under Medicaid at the regular matching rate. These children retain their entitlement to Medicaid benefits (even if SCHIP itself terminates) unless the state changes its eligibility requirements so that they no longer meet the statespecific income, resource and categorical eligibility criteria. States operating separate state programs under SCHIP may cap their enrollment or otherwise restrict participation to limit spending and stay within their capped allotment.

[3] Title XXI of the Social Security Act allows states to use the following factors in determining eligibility: geography, age, income and resources, residency, disability status (so long as any standard relating to that status does not restrict eligibility), access to other health insurance, and duration of SCHIP enrollment. Title XXI funds cannot be used for children who would have been eligible for the state's Medicaid plan under the eligibility standards that were in effect prior to June 1, 1997 or for children covered by a group health plan or other insurance. Under limited circumstances, states have the option to purchase a health benefits plan that is provided by a community-based health delivery system, or to purchase family coverage under a group health plan as long as it is cost-effective to do so.

across states. Allotment of funds among the states is determined by a formula set in law. This grant allotment formula is based on a combination of factors that include the number of low-income children and low-income, uninsured children in the state, and a cost factor that represents average health service industry wages in the state compared to the national average.[4]

These allotments represent federal matching grants available to each state. Like Medicaid, SCHIP is a federal-state matching program. For each dollar of state spending, the federal government will make a matching payment. The SCHIP matching formula is based on the Medicaid matching formula, but results in higher federal matching rates that ranged from 65% to 83.26% in FY2002. FY2002 federal matching rates in Medicaid ranged from 50% to 76.09% of the federal poverty level (FPL).

Funds not drawn down from a state's federal allotment by the end of each fiscal year continue to be available for 2 additional fiscal years, providing each state a total of 3 years to draw down its allotment of federal matching funds for a given fiscal year. For example, FY2003 allotments are available through FY2005. A state must draw down its entire allotment from a given fiscal year before it may access the next year's funding. Under SCHIP law as enacted in 1997, allotments not spent by the end of the applicable 3-year period will be redistributed — by a method to be determined by the Secretary of Health and Human Services (HHS) — to states that have fully spent their original allotments for that year. Redistributed funds not spent by the end of the fiscal year in which they are reallocated will officially expire.[5]

During the 106th Congress, some Members argued that unspent SCHIP funds should be redirected toward other needs. Based on actual and projected spending through February 2000, CMS estimated that $1.9 billion would remain unspent from states' FY1998 allotments. At that time it was too early to tell how much of the FY1999 allotments would also go unspent. Pressures to remain within discretionary spending caps established in the Balanced

---

[4] For a more detailed description of the SCHIP funding process see CRS Report RL30642, *The State Children's Health Insurance Program: Eligibility, Enrollment, and Program Funding*, by Evelyne Baumrucker.

[5] SCHIP law requires that unspent funds remaining at the end of the year in which they are redistributed are no longer available for expenditure by states in the SCHIP program. In generating its baseline estimates, CBO treats unspent redistributions as funds that have reverted to the Treasury. For example, if Congress were to act to continue the availability of expired FY1998 and FY1999 reallocated funds, regardless of whether they legislate on, or after Sept. 30, 2002 (the expiration date of such funds), restoring unspent reallocated funds to the SCHIP program would be treated as a "cost" for the purpose of generating the CBO baseline.

Budget Act of 1997 (BBA 97) led to proposals during 2000 to use unspent SCHIP funds for other purposes. Late in the second session of the 106th Congress (2000), however, it became clear that Congress would not redirect unspent SCHIP funds to other discretionary spending programs. Instead, legislation was enacted that created a special rule for the redistribution of unused FY1998 and FY1999 SCHIP allotments.[6]

The Medicare, Medicaid and SCHIP Benefits Improvement and Protection Act of 2000 (BIPA-2000), incorporated by reference into P.L. 106-554, created a special rule for the redistribution and availability of unused FY1998 and FY1999 SCHIP allotments. The rule decreased the amount available for redistribution to states that had spent all of their allotments by allowing states that had not spent all of their allotments to retain some of their unspent funds.

States that *did* use all their SCHIP FY1998 and FY1999 allotments by the applicable 3-year deadline received an amount equal to their actual spending over that 3-year period in excess of their original exhausted allotment. From remaining unspent funds, states that did *not* use all their SCHIP allotments by the applicable 3- year deadline received an amount equal to their proportional contribution to the total pool of unspent funds. Redistributed and retained funds from FY1998 and FY1999 were made available through the end of FY2002.[7]

At the close of FY2002, unspent FY2000 original allotments were subject to redistribution and unspent BIPA-2000 reallocations (i.e., unspent FY1998 and FY1999 allotments) expired. In reaction to these events, during the 107th Congress, the Senate passed legislation (*The Beneficiary Access to Care and Medicare Equity Act of 2002,* S. 3018) to change the method by which unspent federal funds would be redistributed among states. This legislation would have established a method for redistributing unspent allotments for FY2000 forward for both those states spending all of their allotments and those that have not. In addition, for FY2004 forward, S. 3018 would have established a caseload stabilization pool to provide certain qualifying states — those whose total cumulative spending through the end of the previous fiscal year exceeded their cumulative original allotments for

---

[6] For more information on SCHIP funding issues in the 106th Congress, see CRS Report RS20628, *The State Children's Health Insurance Program (SCHIP): Funding Changes in the 106th Congress,* by Evelyne P. Baumrucker.

[7] For more detail on changes to SCHIP made by BIPA-2000 see CRS Report RL30718, Medicaid, SCHIP, and Other Health Provisions in H.R. 5661: Medicare, Medicaid, and SCHIP Benefits Improvement and Protection Act of 2000, by Jean Hearne, Lisa Herz, and Evelyne Baumrucker.

the same time period — with additional SCHIP funding. Any remaining unspent reallocated dollars beginning with the FY1998 reallocation would have become a part of this pool. In addition, the bill specified that unspent funds in the pool would have remained in the pool (i.e., they would never expire) and would be available for future redistribution to qualifying states. Although bills were introduced in the House regarding SCHIP financing, no further action occurred.

On March 27, 2003, CMS published an interim policy for a partial redistribution of unused FY2000 allotments (available for redistribution after September 30, 2002). The interim redistribution was limited to approximately one-half of the unexpended FY2000 allotments ($1.03 billion) and was targeted to states, commonwealths, and territories that fully spent such allotments by the end of FY2002. Absent a statutory change, the Secretary of HHS is required to redistribute unspent funds *only* to states that exhausted their FY2000 allotments by the required deadline. CMS intended to issue a final redistribution methodology (as determined by the Secretary) in the *Federal Register* by June 30, 2003, unless Congress passed legislation for the redistribution of unspent FY2000 allotments.[8] CMS did not follow through with the publication of a final redistribution methodology when it became clear that SCHIP financing issues were being addressed by the 108th Congress.

Schip Section 1115 Waivers

In the meantime, several states have sought approval for special waivers of SCHIP rules to create additional opportunities to fully spend their SCHIP allotments. Under Section 1115 of the Social Security Act, the Secretary of HHS has broad statutory authority to conduct research and demonstration projects under six programs, including Medicaid and SCHIP. On August 4, 2001 the Bush Administration announced the Health Insurance Flexibility and Accountability (HIFA)1115 Waiver Initiative. This initiative encourages states to develop statewide projects that coordinate Medicaid and SCHIP with private health insurance coverage and target uninsured individuals with income below 200% of the federal poverty level, just as SCHIP does. Later, President Bush indicated that unspent SCHIP funds could be used to finance

---

[8] Centers for Medicare and Medicaid Services (CMS) Letter to State Medicaid Directors and State Health Officials (SMDL #03-003), Mar. 27, 2003. (See **Appendix 2** for interim redistribution payment amounts for unexpended FY2000 SCHIP allotments.)

the HIFA initiative.[9] SCHIP funds are a major source of funding for the approved HIFA waiver projects.

As of May 22, 2003, CMS approved 14 SCHIP 1115 waivers (four others are in review).[10] Seven of the 14 approved waivers are SCHIP HIFA demonstrations. Several of the approvals allow states to use SCHIP funds to cover new groups of individuals such as: pregnant women; parents of SCHIP and Medicaid-eligible children; and childless adults. In three states, Wisconsin, Minnesota, and Rhode Island, the Administration approved a "buy out" of these states' existing Medicaid Section 1115 waivers. That is, in these states certain adult populations that were initially covered under the state's existing Medicaid Section 1115 demonstrations are now covered by SCHIP Section 1115 waiver programs. The approval of these projects as SCHIP demonstrations shifted the funding source from Title XIX funds matched at the regular federal medical assistance percentage (FMAP), to Title XXI allotments matched at the enhanced FMAP. Furthermore, in the case of Arizona and Rhode Island, HHS approved use of SCHIP reallocated funds for coverage of certain adult groups under its SCHIP Section 1115 waiver. All of these waiver approvals have implications for SCHIP financing as they expand the categories of eligibles and circumstances under which capped SCHIP funds may be used.

In a July 2002 report to Congress titled, *Medicaid and SCHIP: Recent HHS Approvals of Demonstration Waiver Projects Raise Concerns,* the General Accounting Office (GAO) expressed concerns that HHS' use of Section 1115 waiver authority to use SCHIP funds to cover childless adults is not consistent with the program's statutory objectives. On August 6, 2002 Senators Baucus and Grassley of the Senate Finance Committee responded to the GAO report by sending a letter to the Secretary of HHS. The Members were concerned that the states' use of SCHIP funds to cover childless adults would result in less money being available for redistribution to states with programs for children.

---

[9] Department of Health and Human Services, Centers For Medicare and Medicaid Services. Report on the Health Insurance Flexibility and Accountability (HIFA) Initiative: State Accessibility to Funding for Coverage Expansions, Oct. 4, 2001.

[10] As of May 22, 2003, 11 states had implemented their SCHIP and HIFA Section 1115 waivers. These states include: Arizona; Colorado; Illinois; Maryland; Minnesota; New Jersey; New Mexico; New York; Oregon; Rhode Island; and Wisconsin.

The Current Debate

SCHIP financing is being revisited by the 108th Congress for a number of reasons. First, 37 states have failed to use all available FY2000 allotments within the 3 years states had to spend that year's funds. These states want continued access to funds that the law requires to be redistributed to states that were able to spend all of their available funds in the given time frame.

Second, 14 states depleted their FY2000 original allotments in the given time frame. Seven of those 14 states spent more than their FY2000 original allotments (state spending for FY2000 may exceed allotments as a result of redistribution of unused FY1998 and FY1999 funds from prior years). These states would like access to unused state allotments, subject to redistribution as required by statute. Absent legislation to redistribute unspent FY2000 allotments, the Secretary would be required to issue a final redistribution methodology that would only benefit this group of states.[11] (See below for a discussion of recent legislative action.)

Third, the *Beneficiary Improvement and Protection Act of 2000* (BIPA-2000) provided access to approximately $4.9 million in unspent redistributed amounts to both groups of states mentioned above. BIPA-2000 decreased the redistribution amount available to states that had exhausted their original allotments for specific years by allowing states that had not spent their full allotments to retain a portion of their unused funds. Even with the continued availability of funds provided by BIPA- 2000, in the aggregate, both groups of states did not manage to spend all the available reallocated funds within the required time periods. State-reported expenditure data through the end of FY2002 show that a majority of states used their redistributed funds, with 19 states failing to do so. Without addressing any additional redistribution of funds, only these 19 states would benefit from the continued availability of the FY1998 and FY1999 reallocated funds. However, most states (above and beyond the 19 states that were unable to deplete their funds) are interested in recouping the $1.3 billion in expired unused FY1998 and FY1999 funding as well as $1.4 billion in unspent funds from the FY2000 redistributions that are projected to expire at the close of FY2003.[12]

Finally, over time, additional states are likely to spend all of their available funds and thus will be eligible for redistributions. FY2002 is the

---

[11] [http://www.cms.gov/states/letters/smd032703.pdf]
[12] Congressional Budget Office (CBO) Mar. 2003 Baseline, *Medicaid and the State Children's Health Insurance Program.* Mar. 11, 2003.

first of 3 years in which the total federal appropriation is 26% less than it was for each of FY1998- FY2001. All states have a vested interest in legislative changes that would increase annual SCHIP appropriations because while more states will be eligible for redistributions, there will be fewer funds available for redistribution to such states. In fact, CMS projects that 15 states will deplete all available SCHIP funds (original and redistributed) over the second half of the program (FY2003-FY2007). States are currently experiencing a period of fiscal distress due to the downturn in the economy since 2000, and they want to be able to sustain the income eligibility limits for their SCHIP programs as the number of uninsured individuals increases.

The 108th Congress has passed redistribution legislation that was signed into law as P.L. 108-74 on August 15, 2003 that attempts to strike a balance between policies to reward fast spending states with the underlying program tenet that SCHIP is a capped grant program under which states must design their programs to stay within budgetary limitations.

SCHIP EXPENDITURE TRENDS

SCHIP Program Expenditures and Enrollment Start Slowly

SCHIP state spending during the first 4 years of the program (FY1998-FY2001) was well below federal appropriations, but has increased over time.[13] For FY1998, SCHIP program federal expenditures totaled $122 million; for FY1999, $922 million; for FY2000, $1.93 billion, and for FY2001 federal expenditures increased to $2.62 billion. This spending trend coincides with enrollment growth. Early enrollment estimates indicated that nearly 1 million children (982,000) were enrolled in SCHIP under 43 operational state programs as of December 1998.[14] SCHIP enrollment grew to nearly 2 million children (1,979,450) under 53 operational programs (in the states, the District of Columbia, and the Outlying Areas) during

---

[13] For each of FY1998 through FY2001, total federal funding available to states and territories was approximately $4.3 billion. For each of FY2002, FY2003, and FY2004, federal funding available to states and territories equals $3.2 billion.

[14] U.S. Health Care Financing Administration, A Preliminary Estimate of the Children's Health Insurance Program Aggregate Enrollment Numbers Through Dec. 31, 1998 (background only), Apr. 20, 1999.

FY1999.[15] The latest official numbers show that total SCHIP enrollment reached 5.3 million children in FY2002. Of this total, 1.3 million participated in SCHIP Medicaid expansions, and 4.0 million children were covered in separate state programs.[16]

FY2002 federal SCHIP expenditures equaled $3.78 billion. This is the first fiscal year in which state spending of available SCHIP funds exceeded the SCHIP program appropriations for that year. In its March 2003 baseline, CBO projected that total federal SCHIP spending will grow to $5.0 billion by FY2007.

State Spending against FY1998-FY2000 Original Allotments

Nationwide, fiscal year account activity across states shows states spent only 52% of the FY1998 original allotments, 34% of the FY1999 original allotments, and 48% of the FY2000 original allotments by their respective deadlines. While most states (including the District of Columbia) failed to spend their original allotments as required within applicable time periods, these states want continued access to funds that the law requires be redistributed to states that were able to spend all of their available funds in the given time frame. (See **Appendix 1** for the state share of original FY1998, FY1999, and FY2000 allotments expended by applicable deadlines.)

As previously described, states and territories are provided annual federal allotments based on a distribution formula set in law. These annual allotments are basically separate, sequential funding accounts. For each state and territory, the account for a given fiscal year is made available at the beginning of that year, and remains available for up to 3 years. SCHIP payments are taken out of the earliest active account. Once that fiscal year allotment is fully expended states can begin to access the next year's allotment, and so forth. Funds remaining in an annual allotment account that was once active for a state, but are no longer available due to the passing of the deadline for availability of such funds, are only available again through the redistribution process.

---

[15] U.S. Health Care Financing Administration, The State Children's Health Insurance Program, Annual Enrollment Report, Oct. 1, 1998- Sept. 30, 1999 (no date).

[16] Centers for Medicare and Medicaid Services, Fiscal Year 2002 Number of Children Ever Enrolled in SCHIP — Preliminary Data Summary, Jan. 30, 2003.

As shown in **Appendix 1**, some states (e.g., Arizona and California) never accessed their FY1999 annual allotments, but did claim against their FY2000 accounts. This was possible because claims against the FY1999 allotments were not made during the 3-year period of availability for such funds. After the deadline for the availability of the FY1999 original allotments (end of FY2001), these states began claiming against the next available account (i.e., FY2000 annual allotments). The same logic applies for states that claimed partial amounts out of a given year's allotment (e.g., Colorado and Connecticut). Such states left a portion of their FY1999 funds unspent at the 3-year deadline (end of FY2001). States are not permitted to access the succeeding year's allotment (in this case, FY2000 funds) until the prior year's allotment (in this case, FY1999 funds) is fully expended, or the deadline for availability of the prior year's funds has passed. In both of the examples above, these states could not begin accessing their FY2000 allotments until FY2002, the final year of availability for FY2000 allotments.

Table 1 illustrates that only a few states spent their original allotments by the relevant deadlines. Before BIPA changes, 12 states would have qualified for redistributions in 1998 and 13 states in 1999. In FY2000, state-reported expenditures through the 4th quarter of FY2002 show that 14 states spent all of their FY2000 allotments by the end of FY2002, as required.[17] These states qualify for the FY2003 redistribution.

Looking at only those 18 states which spent all of their allotments in at least one year during FY1998 through FY2000, eight states qualified for redistributions for each of fiscal years 1998, 1999, and 2000; three states qualified for FY1998 and FY1999 redistributions only; and two states qualified for FY1999 and FY2000 redistributions only. Of the remaining states one additional state received redistributed funds from the FY1998 account only; and state-reported expenditures through the fourth quarter of FY2002 show that four new states will qualify for the FY2000 redistributions only (see **Table 1**).

There are many factors that affect state spending (e.g., state-specific eligibility criteria, outreach and enrollment initiatives, the delivery system used to provide beneficiaries with coverage, or the composition of the

---

[17] For each of FY1998, FY1999, and FY2000 all five territories also spent all of their allotments by the given deadlines. They qualified for the redistribution of unspent funds from these accounts.

benefit package available to beneficiaries). These differences help to explain the variation in spending among states.

Table 1. Redistribution States for Each of FY1998 through FY2000

State	FY1998	FY1999	FY2000
Alaska	x	x	x
Indiana	x	x	
Kansas			x
Kentucky	x	x	x
Maine	x	x	x
Maryland	x	x	x
Massachusetts	x	x	x
Minnesota			x
Mississippi			x
Missouri	x	x	
New Jersey		x	x
New York	x	x	x
North Carolina	x	x	
Pennsylvania	x		
Rhode Island	x	x	x
South Carolina	x	x	x
West Virginia			x
Wisconsin		x	x
Five Territories	x	x	x
Total States Only	12	13	14

Source: *Federal Register*, vol. 66, no. 120, June 21, 2001, p. 33263 and *Federal Register*, vol. 67, no. 81, Apr. 26, 2002, p. 20799, and Centers for Medicare and Medicaid Services, 4th quarter FY2002 state-reported expenditure data.

Note: Shaded cells with an "x" represent states that spent their original allotments by the relevant deadlines and thus qualified for a redistribution of unused funds from prior years. All five territories (Puerto Rico, Guam, Virgin Islands, American Samoa, and Northern Mariana Islands) also received redistributed funds in each of FY1998 through FY2000.

Congress Reacts to Early Program Expenditure Trends Through Enactment of the BIPA-2000 Reallocation

The Beneficiary Improvement and Protection Act of 2000 (BIPA-2000) provided access to unspent reallocated amounts for both groups of states mentioned above (i.e., states that spent more than their original allotments in the given time period and states that were not able to use all available allotments within applicable time periods). BIPA-2000 decreased the amount available for redistribution to states that had exhausted their original allotments for specific years by allowing states that had not spent their full allotments to retain a portion of their unused funds.

The method for providing access to BIPA-2000 reallocated funds is different from that used for original allotments. CMS permitted states to access reallocated funds from FY1998 during FY2001 and FY2002, and reallocated funds from FY1999 during FY2002 (at which point remaining unused funds reverted to the Treasury). These reallocated funds became additional active accounts whose availability overlapped with other original allotments. Thus, during FY2001 and FY2002 only, states could draw federal matching funds from more than one active account (for example, FY2001 original allotments and FY1998 reallocated funds).

Table 2 shows SCHIP expenditures against open allotments through September 2002. During this reporting period, 5 fiscal year accounts — FY1998 through FY2002 — were available to states.[18] These accounts include: (1) FY1998 reallocated funds; (2) FY1999 reallocated funds; (3) FY2000 original allotments; (4) FY2001 original allotments; and (5) FY2002 original allotments. During FY2001 and FY2002 only, two of the above-listed accounts could be active simultaneously (one original allotment and one account containing reallocated funds).

The first five columns of **Table 2** show the percentage of each of the available active accounts that states spent by the end of FY2002 (shaded cells containing " — "indicate a depleted account; blank cells indicate that the fiscal year account was not accessed). FY2002 expenditure data show that 47 states (including the District of Columbia) depleted their FY1998 reallocated funds. Only 5% ($102.2 million) of the FY1998 reallocated funds remained at the close of FY2002. By contrast, for the FY1999 reallocations, 32 states (including the District of Columbia) depleted their available funds leaving an unspent balance of 41% ($1.2 billion) of available funds by the deadline. In total, states spent 74% of the $4.9 billion available through the

---

[18] Federal fiscal years run from Oct. 1 through Sept. 30 and are labeled according to the calendar year in which they end. So for example, FY2002 began on Oct. 1, 2001 and ended on Sept. 30, 2002. Under SCHIP, FY1998 funds were available through the end of FY2000 (Sept. 30, 2000). FY1999 funds were available through the end of FY2001 (Sept. 30, 2001). Unspent funds for these 2 fiscal years were redistributed as authorized under BIPA (described above). FY2000 funds were available through FY2002, and FY2001 funds are available through FY2003.

BIPA-2000 reallocations, leaving an unspent balance of $1.3 billion by the close of FY2002 (see **Appendix 2**).

Like state spending against original allotments, the BIPA-2000 reallocations continued the availability of unused prior year funding at levels higher than many states were able to spend (in the allowable time periods). In fact, during this 5-year reporting period only five of the 14 states that spent all of their FY1998 and/or FY1999 allotments had cumulative expenditures that exceeded their cumulative original allotments and thus, were required to rely on BIPA-2000 redistributed funds as allowed in statute to finance their program expenditures.[19] However, with the addition of the BIPA-2000 redistributed funds to their available original allotments, these five states also have unspent funds remaining at the end of FY2002 (**Table 2** last column). Expenditure data through the end of FY2002 show that without a legislative change to require an additional re-allotment of the BIPA-2000 reallocated funds, only 19 states would benefit from a proposal to continue the availability of unspent funds (See **Table 2**).

Most states (above and beyond the 19 states that were unable to deplete their funds) are also interested in recouping BIPA-2000 funds as well as approximately $1.4 billion that are expected to expire at the end of FY2003. These states would prefer to see redistribution legislation that would channel unused prior year program funding to states whose expenditure and enrollment data show that such states could make use of prior year program funds. While the continued availability of unused prior year funds and an additional redistribution process may better direct existing SCHIP resources to states that choose to expand their SCHIP programs to maximize coverage to new (or existing) groups of uninsured individuals, a recycling of unused SCHIP program funds in this way may be perceived as creating an incentive for states to capture additional federal dollars by spending more than is available through their original allotments. However, states relying on redistributed funds to finance their SCHIP programs may not be able to sustain their programs in future years when less funds are available for redistribution to qualifying states.

---

[19] These states include: (1) Alaska; (2) Maryland; (3) New Jersey; (4) New York; and (5) Rhode Island.

State Spending against all Available Funds, FY1998-FY2002

In addition to state spending against the BIPA-2000 reallocated funds, the last four columns of **Table 2** map state spending against *all* available funds during this 5-year reporting period, FY1998 through FY2002. The second to last column of **Table 2** shows the percentage of *all* available funds each state spent by the end of FY2002. **Figure 1** displays these percentages graphically and ranks states according to their spending of all available allotments (original and reallocated). States that appear on the right hand side of this figure were more likely to qualify for redistributions in each of FY1998-FY2000. While redistributed funds are available, assuming current expenditure trends, these "high spending" states may begin to rely on redistributed funds to finance their programs in future years.

By the end of FY2002, expenditure data indicates that 29 states (including the District of Columbia) spent less than half of their available funds. Of those 29 states, eight spent less than 25% of their available cumulative funds and 21 states (including the District of Columbia) spent between 25% and 50% of their available funds.

Of the 22 states that spent more than 50% of available funds for FY1998 through FY2002, 20 states spent between 50% and 75%, and two states (New Jersey and Rhode Island) spent more than three-quarters of all available funds by the end of FY2002. Further, only seven states accessed their FY2001 allotments. By the end of FY2002, Rhode Island was the only state to deplete its FY2001 allotment and access its FY2002 allotment. Nationally, as seen in the last row of **Table 2**, expenditure data show that states spent approximately 46.9% of all available federal funds by the end of FY2002, leaving an unspent balance of approximately $10.7 billion from the FY1998 through FY2002 allotments. Of that total, approximately $2.2 billion of the unspent FY2000 funds are available for redistribution in FY2003.

Table 2. SCHIP Program Allotments and Expenditures by State, FY1998-FY2002 (in thousands)

State	Percent of each active available account spent (through 9/30/02)					Total available (adjusted)[a] allotment amounts for FY1998-FY2002	Total expenditures applied against allotments (through 9/30/02)	Percent of available (adjusted)[a] allotments spent (through 9/30/02)	Allotment balance at end of FY2002[b]
	1998 reallocated	1999 reallocated	2000	2001	2002				
Alabama	—	—	37.4%			$ 320,043	$ 153,953	48.1%	$ 166,090
Alaska #†ˢ	—	54.4%	—			$ 91,051	$ 66,482	73.0%	$ 24,569
Arizona	—	—	57.8%			$ 479,610	$ 213,005	44.4%	$ 266,605
Arkansas	13.6%	—	—			$ 195,714	$ 6,213	3.2%	$ 189,501
California	—	—	3.0%			$ 2,998,522	$ 1,022,659	34.1%	$ 1,975,864
Colorado	—	—	37.7%			$ 184,182	$ 76,067	41.3%	$ 108,115
Connecticut	—	35.0%	11.3%			$ 154,601	$ 54,410	35.2%	$ 100,191
Delaware	—	—	—			$ 37,435	$ 7,190	19.2%	$ 30,245
District of Columbia	—	—	9.9%			$ 46,358	$ 17,008	36.7%	$ 29,349
Florida	—	—	89.0%			$ 1,059,194	$ 648,261	61.2%	$ 410,933
Georgia	—	—	51.1%			$ 543,921	$ 239,137	44.0%	$ 304,784
Hawaii	—	38.5%	—			$ 40,828	$ 7,363	18.0%	$ 33,465
Idaho	—	—	69.2%			$ 83,117	$ 40,113	48.3%	$ 43,005
Illinois	—	60.3%	—			$ 573,738	$ 128,896	22.5%	$ 444,842
Indiana #†	—	—	79.5%			$ 461,019	$ 235,787	51.1%	$ 225,232
Iowa	—	—	73.9%			$ 143,700	$ 79,904	55.6%	$ 63,797
Kansas ˢ	—	—	—	2.3%		$ 132,745	$ 82,104	61.9%	$ 50,641
Kentucky #†ˢ	—	35.7%	—			$ 374,247	$ 217,915	58.2%	$ 156,333
Louisiana	—	—	21.6%			$ 351,625	$ 140,437	39.9%	$ 211,188
Maine #†ˢ	—	29.5%	—			$ 85,592	$ 48,956	57.2%	$ 36,636
Maryland #†ˢ	—	68.5%	—			$ 446,975	$ 318,362	71.2%	$ 128,613
Massachusetts #†ˢ	—	22.3%	—			$ 358,621	$ 189,717	52.9%	$ 168,904
Michigan	—	—	6.1%			$ 441,650	$ 128,810	29.2%	$ 312,840

State	Percent of each active available account spent (through 9/30/02)					Total available (adjusted)[a] allotment amounts for FY1998-FY2002	Total expenditures applied against allotments (through 9/30/02)	Percent of available (adjusted)[a] allotments spent (through 9/30/02)	Allotment balance at end of FY2002[b]
	1998 reallocated	1999 reallocated	2000	2001	2002				
Minnesota	—	—	—	—	—	$ 129,139	$ 65,423	50.7%	$ 63,716
Mississippi[‡]	—	—	—	9.1%	—	$ 240,217	$ 147,912	61.6%	$ 92,305
Missouri [#†]	—	—	2.2%	2.9%	—	$ 343,483	$ 175,404	51.1%	$ 168,080
Montana	—	—	84.6%	—	—	$ 58,964	$ 30,839	52.3%	$ 28,125
Nebraska	—	—	49.6%	—	—	$ 72,741	$ 31,138	42.8%	$ 41,603
Nevada	—	—	29.9%	—	—	$ 128,342	$ 47,977	37.4%	$ 80,365
New Hampshire	—	23.3%	—	—	—	$ 44,369	$ 9,413	21.2%	$ 34,956
New Jersey [†‡]	—	—	—	78.2%	—	$ 542,408	$ 451,398	83.2%	$ 91,009
New Mexico [#†]	57.8%	—	—	—	—	$ 209,107	$ 26,128	12.5%	$ 182,979
New York [#†‡]	—	23.9%	—	—	—	$ 2,517,549	$ 1,405,833	55.8%	$ 1,111,716
North Carolina [#†]	—	—	87.2%	—	—	$ 545,750	$ 257,313	47.1%	$ 288,437
North Dakota	—	—	33.6%	—	—	$ 23,829	$ 8,164	34.3%	$ 15,664
Ohio	—	—	90.7%	—	—	$ 589,150	$ 326,767	55.5%	$ 262,383
Oklahoma	—	88.1%	—	—	—	$ 302,822	$ 107,317	35.4%	$ 195,505
Oregon	—	—	2.3%	—	—	$ 181,828	$ 51,227	28.2%	$ 130,601
Pennsylvania [#]	—	—	74.9%	—	—	$ 588,656	$ 317,709	54.0%	$ 270,947
Rhode Island [#†‡]	—	—	—	—	39.7%	$ 70,031	$ 65,522	93.6%	$ 4,510
South Carolina [#†‡]	15.3%	—	—	—	—	$ 437,593	$ 206,138	47.1%	$ 231,455
South Dakota	—	—	78.4%	—	—	$ 34,379	$ 18,542	53.9%	$ 15,836
Tennessee	—	9.6%	—	—	—	$ 307,585	$ 60,139	19.6%	$ 247,446
Texas	—	—	50.8%	—	—	$ 1,882,714	$ 881,015	46.8%	$ 1,001,700
Utah	—	—	89.2%	—	—	$ 125,376	$ 69,232	55.2%	$ 56,143
Vermont	—	—	41.1%	—	—	$ 17,536	$ 6,848	39.0%	$ 10,688
Virginia	—	—	—	—	—	$ 284,710	$ 92,210	32.4%	$ 192,500
Washington	45.6%	—	15.3%	—	—	$ 205,491	$ 14,180	6.9%	$ 191,310

State	Percent of each active available account spent (through 9/30/02)					Total available (adjusted)[a] allotment amounts for FY1998-FY2002	Total expenditures applied against allotments (through 9/30/02)	Percent of available (adjusted)[a] allotments spent (through 9/30/02)	Allotment balance at end of FY2002[b]
	1998 reallocated	1999 reallocated	2000	2001	2002				
West Virginia[c]	—	—	—	8.2%	—	$ 95,929	$ 59,860	62.4%	$ 36,069
Wisconsin [†][‡]	—	—	—	—	—	$ 248,170	$ 159,327	64.2%	$ 88,843
Wyoming	—	56.3%	—	—	—	$ 28,126	$ 7,160	25.5%	$ 20,966
MOE[c]	NOT APPLICABLE					$ 7,894	NOT APPLICABLE		$ 7,894
Puerto Rico [#][†][‡]	—	—	—	—	1.9%	$ 208,136	$ 178,424	1.9%	$ 29,711
Guam [#][†][‡]	—	—	—	20.8%	—	$ 7,953	$ 5,550	69.8%	$ 2,403
Virgin Islands [#][†][‡]	—	—	—	83.0%	—	$ 5,908	$ 4,079	69.1%	$ 1,828
American Samoa [#][†][‡]	—	—	—	—	—	$ 2,727	$ 4,128	151.4%	$ (1,401)
N. Mariana Isl. [#][†][‡]	—	—	—	—	—	$ 2,499	$ 5,203	208.2%	$ (2,704)
Total (all states and territories)	95.0%	58.9%	48.2%	3.4%	0.0%	$ 20,095,600	$ 9,420,272	46.9%	$ 10,675,328

Source: Centers for Medicare and Medicaid Services, 4th quarter FY2002 state-reported expenditure data as of Nov. 30, 2002. (From unpublished reports: FY02RPT.xls, CHIP1202.xls and ST121602.xls).

Note: Shaded cells with " — " represent depleted accounts at the close of FY2002 as reported to CMS by Nov. 30, 2002. Blank cells represent available accounts that have not been accessed by the states at the close of FY2002 as reported to CMS by Nov. 30, 2002.

[a] "Adjusted" refers to increases or decreases to the amounts provided by states' original FY1998 and FY1999 allotments due to the redistribution of unspent FY1998 and FY1999 funds. For states that received redistributions of other states' unspent funds, this amount is greater than what was provided by original allotments. For states that contributed unspent funds to the pool for redistribution for other states, this amount is less than what was provided by original allotments (the amount is derived by subtracting out the unspent funds and adding back the amount the state was able to retain due to BIPA-2000).

[b] This is NOT the amount that will be available to states in FY2003. To derive that amount, the following adjustments need to be made to the number in this column: 1) subtract the amount of unspent FY1998 and FY1999 reallocated funds that expired Sept. 30, 2002 under current law; 2) add in redistributions of unspent FY2000 funds (amounts will depend on whether Congress acts to create a redistribution method, as it did in BIPA-2000; if Congress does not act, the amount will depend on the method CMS chooses for redistribution); and 3) add in new allotments for FY2003.

a. MOE refers to one of the maintenance of effort provisions in SCHIP statute. When SCHIP was created, three states — Florida, New York and Pennsylvania — had existing comprehensive state-based health benefit programs for children that were deemed to meet SCHIP requirements. These states are required to maintain their prior level of spending under SCHIP. Specifically, beginning in FY1999, the allotment for a given fiscal year will be reduced by the difference between the state's spending in the prior fiscal year versus FY1996 (before SCHIP began). The $7.9 million shown for MOE in this table reflects spending patterns in Pennsylvania for FY1999, in which Pennsylvania's share of SCHIP costs was $7.9 million less than FY1996 spending, so its allotment for FY2000 has been reduced by $7.9 million. This amount will be included in the redistribution process for FY2000. (Pennsylvania's share of FY1998 SCHIP costs was $2.2 million less than FY1996 spending, and its SCHIP allotment for FY1999 was reduced by $2.2 million. This amount is not shown in the MOE cell because it has already been redistributed to other states in the FY1998 redistribution process.)

\# indicates the 12 states that fully expended their original FY1998 allotments by the end of FY2000 as required, and therefore received additional "redistributed" FY1998 funds. All five territories (Puerto Rico, Guam, Virgin Islands, American Samoa, and Northern Mariana Islands) also received redistributed FY1998 funds. The remaining 39 states (including the District of Columbia) did not spend their full FY1998 allotments by the end of FY2000. Such states received a "retained allotment" amount in the FY1998 redistribution process.

† indicates the 13 states that fully expended their original FY1999 allotments by the end of FY2001 as required, and therefore received additional "redistributed" FY1999 funds (see text for explanation). All five territories (Puerto Rico, Guam, Virgin Islands, American Samoa, and Northern Mariana Islands) also received redistributed FY1999 funds. The remaining 38 states (including the District of Columbia) did not spend their full FY1999 allotments by the end of FY2001. Such states received a "retained allotment" amount in the FY1999 redistribution process.

§ State-reported expenditure data predicts 14 states to have fully expended their original FY2000 allotments by the end of FY2002 as required, and therefore they will receive additional "redistributed" FY2000 funds (see text for explanation). Expenditure data also indicates that all five territories (Puerto Rico, Guam, Virgin Islands, American Samoa, and Northern Mariana Islands) will receive redistributed FY2000 funds. The remaining 37 states (including the District of Columbia) did not spend their full FY2000 allotments by the end of FY2002. Such states received a "retained allotment" amount in the FY2000 redistribution process. The identification of the FY2000 redistribution and retention states are based CRS analysis of state-reported expenditure data submitted to CMS as of Nov. 30, 2002.

* See *footnote a* of **Table 1** for an explanation of "adjusted."

Figure 1. FY1998-2002 Spending as a Percentage of FY1998-2002 Available (Adjusted)* Funds

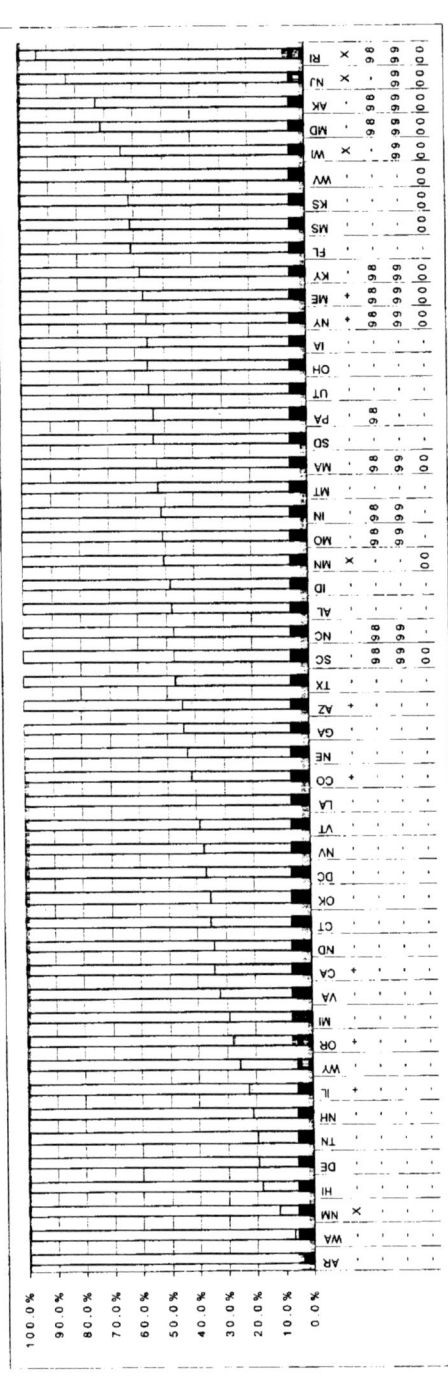

Source: CRS analysis of FY2002 state-reported expenditure data through Sept. 30, 2003, as reported to CMS on Form 21-C by Nov. 30, 2002.
Note: Under each state abbreviation, an 'X' identifies states with an SCHIP Section 1115 waiver that covers one or more categories of adults and was implemented as of Sept. 30, 2002. For such states, some portion of the spending shown on this chart is associated with service spending for adults. A '+' identifies states with an approved SCHIP Section 1115 waiver (as of Apr. 11, 2003) that covers one or more categories of adults, but was *not* implemented as of September 30, 2002 [http://www.cms.gov/schip/1115waiv.pdf]. For such states, *none* of the spending shown on this chart is associated with service spending for adults since the programs were not implemented as of the end of FY2002. States with "98," "99," and "00" indicated whether the state qualified for a redistribution for each of FY1998, FY1999, and FY2000 respectively.

Spending Trends over the Life of the Program May Shape the Future of SCHIP Financing

Over time, more and more states are likely to spend all of their available funds and thus will be eligible for redistributions. FY2002 is the first of 3 years in which the total federal appropriation is 26% less than it was for each of FY1998-FY2001. Often referred to as the "SCHIP dip," this decrease in appropriations was written into SCHIP's authorizing legislation due to budgetary constraints at that time. While additional states will be eligible for redistributions, fewer funds will be available for redistribution to such states. These states may not be able to sustain the high levels of spending they achieved when more program funds were available. CMS projects shortfalls for 15 states over the second half of the program (FY2003-2007). In most cases, these states are expected to spend all of their allotments and to rely on redistributed funds, but not have sufficient redistributed funds to operate at their October 2001 levels.

To illustrate this point, on the national level, **Table 3** provides a variety of point-in-time and cumulative statistics on annual allotments and expenditure patterns over the life of the SCHIP program, FY1998 — FY2007. **Table 3** captures the complexity of SCHIP financing inherent in the statutory and regulatory requirements governing this program (i.e., the 3-year availability of original allotments, the continued availability of unused prior year funds for redistribution among qualifying states, BIPA-2000's special rule for the continued availability of unused FY1998 and FY1999 allotments, as well as the order and time frame by which states may access each available account). The role of **Table 3** is to visualize the interplay of each of these financing requirements over the life of the program using actual expenditure data for FY1998 through FY2002 and CBO March 2003 Baseline estimates for FY2003 through FY2007.

FY1998-FY2001: New Allotments Exceed Spending

As seen in **Table 3**, in FY1998, states spent only 2.9% (sixth row) of the FY1998 allotment. In fact, only 19 states spent any SCHIP funds during FY1998, and only two of them — New York and South Carolina — spent more than 10% of their state-specific allotments (data not shown) in that year. This meant that $4.113 billion (fifth row) of the FY1998 allotment was carried forward for use in FY1999. An additional $4.247 billion in FY1999 original allotments was also available to states (first row).

During FY1999, all states except five[20] spent at least some SCHIP funds. State spending in that year totaled 11.0% (sixth row) of available funds. (Available funds consisted of unspent FY1998 allotments and the new FY1999 allotment). Because states may not use a given year's allotment until it has depleted the previous fiscal year's allotment (or the previous year's allotment is no longer available), states drew nearly all of FY1999 expenditures from the FY1998 allotments.[21] At the end of FY1999, $7.438 billion (fifth row) in unspent SCHIP funds carried forward for use in FY2000.

By the end of FY2000, all states were claiming SCHIP funds. State spending for the year totaled 16.5% (sixth row) of available funds. (Available funds consisted of unspent FY1998 and FY1999 allotments and the new FY2000 allotment). The fifth row shows that $9.759 billion in unspent funds carried forward for state access in FY2001. Just over 2 billion dollars ($2.034 billion, row 5b) of the unspent funds that carried forward for state use in FY2001 were FY1998 reallocated funds.

In FY2001, spending for the year came to 19.1% (sixth row) of available funds, and $11.336 billion (fifth row) of unspent funds carried forward for state use in FY2002. Almost 3 billion dollars ($2.819 billion, row 5b) of unspent funds that carried forward for state use in FY2002 were FY1999 reallocated funds. The remainder of the unspent funds ($8.517 billion, row 5a) included: (1) unspent FY2000 and FY2001 allotments; as well as (2) unspent FY1998 reallocated funds that states were permitted to use for an extra year under BIPA-2000.

FY2002 Through FY2007: State Expenditures Exceed Annual Appropriations

FY2002 is the first year that total spending exceeds that year's appropriation (reflected by the negative value in the third row of **Table 3**).[22] Thus, it is in FY2002 that states' SCHIP balances begin to decline as new annual allotments cannot keep pace with states' increased program spending. This trend is predicted to continue through the remainder of the program as more and more states deplete their original allotments. Assessing current

---

[20] Hawaii, Oklahoma, Tennessee, Washington, and Wyoming.
[21] New York and South Carolina were the only states to finish their FY1998 allotments during FY1999. These states began accessing their FY1999 allotments in that year.
[22] State-reported expenditure data through the fourth quarter of FY2002 show federal SCHIP expenditures reached $3.78 billion. This exceeds the FY2002 appropriations by $661 million.

program trends, these states must turn to other available funds (i.e., redistributed funds) to finance their programs.

Two other factors contribute to the decline of nationwide SCHIP balances and the related acceleration in "spending as a share of available funds" between FY2002 (26.1%) and FY2004 (49.7%), (sixth row). First, FY2002 is the first of 3 years in which total federal appropriations are 26% less than annual levels for fiscal years 1998-2001 (first row). Because the "SCHIP dip" results in less new money available to states, it also contributes to a more rapid decline in the nationwide balance of unused funds.

Second, FY2002 state-reported expenditure data shows almost $1.3 billion from the BIPA-2000 reallocation expired at the end of FY2002 (row 5c). At the end of FY2003, CBO estimates that $1.4 billion in unspent FY2000 funds will expire (row 5c). According to CBO, no funds are expected to expire in FY2004 or beyond (row 5c). Thus approximately $9.416 billion in unspent funds carry forward from FY2002 to FY2003. (These include $10.675 billion (fifth row) minus $1.259 billion in expiring funds — row 5c.) Part of the funds that carry forward from FY2002 to FY2003 will be comprised of FY2000 redistributed funds (row 5b) as well as unused FY2001 and FY2002 allotments (row 5a). **Figure 2** shows the data presented in **Table 3** graphically.

For FY2003 and beyond, spending nationally is projected to exceed annual allotments each year, so the unused balance carried forward over time will decrease (fifth row). A significant decrease in the unspent balance is projected to occur at the end of FY2003 due to CBO's predicted expiration of approximately $1.4 billion in FY2000 redistributed funds (row 5c). Unspent balances carrying forward from FY2003 to FY2004 will be approximately $6.691 billion ($8.091 billion (fifth row) minus the $1.4 billion CBO estimates to expire — row 5c).

Table 3. Allotments and Actual and Projected
Available Funds and Spending, FY1998-2007 (in millions)

	Actual expenditures*						Projected expenditures**			
	1998	1999	2000	2001	2002	2003	2004	2005	2006	2007
(1) Allotment	$4,235	$4,247	$4,249	$4,249	$3,115	$3,175	$3,175	$4,082	$4,082	$5,040
(2) Spending	$122	$922	$1,929	$2,672	$3,776	$4,500	$4,900	$4,700	$4,700	$5,000
(3) Allotment in excess of spending	$4,113	$3,325	$2,320	$1,578	($661)	($1,325)	($1,725)	($618)	($618)	$40
(4) Total funds available this year	$4,235	$8,360	$11,688	$14,008	$14,452	$12,591	$9,867	$9,049	$8,431	$8,771
(5) Available unspent funds	$4,113	$7,438	$9,759	$11,336	$10,675	$8,091	$4,967	$4,349	$3,731	$3,771
(5a) Original allotments not yet subject to reallocation	$4,113	$7,438	$7,725	$8,517	$7,210	$5,991	$4,767	$4,249	$3,631	$3,671
(5b) Original allotments subject to reallocation	—	—	$2,034	$2,819	$2,206	$700	$200	$100	$100	$100
(5c) Expiring funds	—	—	—	—	$1,259	$1,400	—	—	—	—
(6) Spending as share of available funds	2.9%	11.0%	16.5%	19.1%	26.1%	35.7%	49.7%	51.9%	55.7%	57.0%
(7) Cumulative funds available since start of program	$4,235	$8,482	$12,731	$16,980	$20,096	$22,012	$23,787	$27,869	$31,952	$36,992
(8) Cumulative spent since start of program	$122	$1,044	$2,972	$5,644	$9,420	$13,920	$18,820	$23,520	$28,220	$33,220
(9) Cumulative spent as share of cumulative funds	2.9%	12.3%	23.3%	33.2%	46.9%	63.2%	79.1%	84.4%	88.3%	89.8%

Notes: The first row shows the national allotment made available to states and territories each year. Allotments include: (1) amounts available to states and territories as specified in BBA 97 at the time of enactment; and (2) adjustments to the total appropriations available for states and territories enacted by P.L. 105-277, and P.L. 106-113. The second row shows each year's spending (*actual spending through 2002 and **CBO *March 2003 Baseline* estimates for 2003 and beyond). The third row shows the amount by which each year's allotment exceeds that year's spending or if spending exceeds the allotment, as it does in FY2002 forward, vice versa.)

Rows four, five, and six show how spending each year relates to the funds available to states that year. The fourth row shows total funding available that year, comprised of: (1) initial annual allotments, (2) any remaining funds carried over from previous years; and (3) starting in FY2001, redistributed funds. The fifth row shows available funds unspent at the end of the year. Row 5a, 5b, and 5c (in italics) show how available unspent funds break out between: (a) available unspent original allotments that are not yet subject to reallocation, (b) available original allotments that are subject to reallocation (i.e., unused prior year funds available for reallocation among qualifying states in the following year), and (c) expiring funds (i.e., FY1998 and FY1999 reallocated funds that were not spent by the end of FY2002, and FY2000 reallocated funds that CBO estimates will not be spent by the end of FY2003). The sum of rows 5a, 5b, and 5c equals the total available unspent funds in row five. The sixth row shows each year's spending as a percentage of funds available that year.

The last three rows show the relationship between cumulative spending and cumulative available funds over the life of the program. Expiring funds are subtracted out of "Cumulative funds available since the start of program" (seventh row) for FY2003 forward.

Figure 2 shows the data presented in this table graphically.

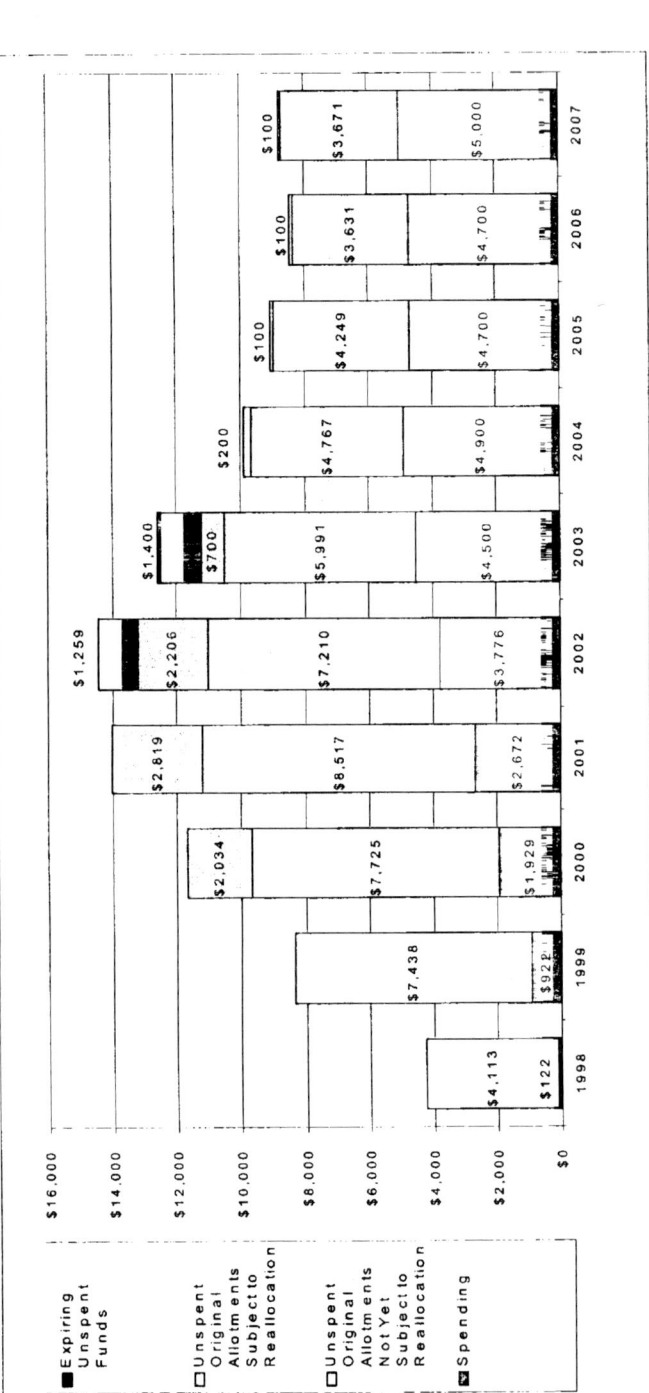

Figure 2. Actual and Projected Available Funds and Spending, FY1998-2007

Notes: This figure portrays available funds and spending each year as shown in **Table 3**. From bottom to top, each bar is comprised of: (1) spending (**Table 3**, second row); (2) unspent original allotments that continue to be available to all states the following year (**Table 3**, row 5a); (3) unspent funds that will be reallocated the following year (**Table 3**, row 5b); and (4) expiring funds for FY2002 and FY2003 only (**Table 3**, row 5c). In any given year each bar represents total funds available for that year (**Table 3**, row 4).

Using CBO estimates without any legislative or policy change, by the end of FY2007, the total unused balance will decline to approximately $3.771 billion (fifth row).[23] Each year, the portion of unspent funds available for redistribution to qualifying states will become smaller (row 5b). However, funds available for redistribution are not expected to disappear completely, since it is likely that some states will never spend all of their allotments by the applicable 3-year deadline.

Variation in SCHIP Spending among States

The extent to which a state will be affected by the shrinking pool of funds available for redistribution depends on the amount by which the state's spending exceeds its available funds. States show an extremely wide variation in the extent to which they utilized their allotments, with some states spending significantly less than their original allotments and some spending more. State spending is directly linked to program enrollment. States have the flexibility to design their SCHIP programs "narrowly" or "broadly" in terms of the pool of eligible individuals. There are many other factors that also affect state spending (e.g., the delivery system used to provide beneficiaries with coverage, or the composition of the benefit package available to beneficiaries).

For instance, New Jersey, which consistently spent a larger share of its allotments than most states, chose an ambitious expansion by extending coverage to children in families with incomes up to 350% FPL. Minnesota and Arkansas, conversely, consistently spent very small shares of their allotments, although for different reasons. Arkansas chose a minimal expansion from its pre-SCHIP Medicaid thresholds. Expenditure data through the end of FY2002 show that Arkansas used the smallest share of its available SCHIP funding to date (3.2%).[24]

---

[23] It is important to note that the estimates in the CBO baseline — like any projections — are limited in their precision, especially in out-years. While the baseline projections take into consideration factors such as inflation, state plan amendments, and spending under Section 1115 waivers, differences between CBO's assumptions and actual program changes over time will result in a difference between CBO projections and actual spending. For example, if actual spending is higher than CBO projections, the balance of unspent funds at the end of FY2007 will be smaller than $3.8 billion. On the other hand, if actual spending is lower than CBO projections, the balance of unspent funds remaining at the end of FY2007 will be greater than $3.8 billion.

[24] CRS Report RL30642, *The State Children's Health Insurance Program: Eligibility, Enrollment, and Program Funding*, by Evelyne Baumrucker includes a table showing

Minnesota, by contrast, had high Medicaid eligibility thresholds prior to SCHIP (275% FPL for all children ages 0-18) and used its SCHIP funds to expand Medicaid to children under age 2 in families with income up to 280% FPL. In FY1999, FY2000, and FY2001, Minnesota enrolled 21, 24, and 49 children, respectively. As of the end of FY2001, Minnesota used an even smaller share of its available SCHIP funding (0.6%) than Arkansas over the same time period. Minnesota's spending increased considerably since the implementation of its Section 1115 SCHIP waiver to cover parents of SCHIP and Medicaid-eligible children. With its operational Section 1115 waiver, at the close of FY2002, state-reported expenditure data show that Minnesota claimed 50.7% of its available funding. (See **Figure 1** for a ranking of cumulative state spending for FY1998-2002 as percentage of FY1998-FY2002 available funds. This figure also identifies states with approved SCHIP Section 1115 waiver programs that cover one or more categories of adults.)

However, even if states have similar program designs, enormous enrollment variability can exist due to the complex interaction between economic trends (e.g., the recent economic downturn will likely increase the number of individuals eligible for SCHIP); federal and state policies (e.g., statewide projects that expand coverage to new groups of uninsured individuals); program administrative procedures (e.g., those that simplify and expedite the eligibility determination and enrollment process); and beneficiary perceptions unique to each state. Each of these factors affect enrollment and influence state spending.

Shortfalls Projected for Some States

Two recent analyses — one by the Centers for Medicare and Medicaid Services (CMS)[25] and the other by the Center on Budget and Policy Priorities (CBPP)[26] use models to forecast which states will face significant federal allotment constraints in out-years. Both models account for state-specific SCHIP funding and expenditures. CBPP uses the same model created by

---

eligibility thresholds under state SCHIP programs as well as states' Medicaid income eligibility thresholds prior to SCHIP.

[25] Centers for Medicare and Medicaid Services, Report on the Health Insurance Flexibility and Accountability (HIFA) Initiative: State Accessibility to Funding for Coverage Expansions, Oct. 4, 2001.

[26] Center on Budget and Policy Priorities. OMB Estimates Indicate That 900,000 Children Will Lose Health Insurance Due to Reductions in Federal SCHIP Funding, Aug. 2, 2002.

CMS' Office of the Actuary (OACT) with modifications. Both analyses define "available funds" to include annual original allotments and additional unspent funds such states are projected to receive through SCHIP redistributions.[27]

CMS and CBPP agree that the same 15 states will exceed all of their available SCHIP funds by FY2006 (**Table 4**), some sooner than others. In addition to the 15 states, CBPP adds Arizona and Louisiana to their list of states who are predicted to exceed their available funding (in FY2005 and FY2006 respectively).[28] The last column of the table indicates states with SCHIP Section 1115 waivers. States with approved waivers are allowed to use SCHIP funds to cover groups not traditionally eligible for SCHIP.

Also captured in **Table 4** is the type of SCHIP program operating in the state. As discussed previously, states with separate state programs have the flexibility to design their programs to operate within current funding constraints. While this may mean that states must cap enrollment or otherwise control spending to stay within their capped federal allotments, targeted low-income children enrolled in Medicaid are entitled to Medicaid benefits as long as they continue to meet state-specific eligibility criteria. These children will have continued access to health insurance coverage unless the state eliminates the new optional Medicaid eligibility category of optional targeted low-income children, or otherwise changes its income, or resource criteria for targeted low-income children covered through an existing Medicaid eligibility category.

---

[27] Each analysis incorporates its own assumption regarding the method for redistribution of unspent funds. CMS calculates projected redistributions of unspent allotments based on an assumption that qualifying states will receive redistributed funds in proportion to original allotments. It is unclear whether CBPP calculates projected redistributions using the BIPA-2000 formula or by another method.

[28] CMS's analysis was released prior to the Dec. 2001 approval of Arizona's HIFA waiver and therefore does not include projected spending associated with the waiver. CMS's analysis projects that by FY2006 Louisiana's expenditures will comprise 81% of its available funds.

Table 4. States Expected to Use All of Their Available SCHIP Funds by FY2006 (CMS and CBPP Projections)

State	First year in which expected to use all available funds	Type of SCHIP program			Has 1115 waiver expanding eligibility to new groups
		Medicaid expansion only	Separate state program only	Combination program	
Alaska	FY2004	X			
Idaho	FY2006	X			
Indiana	FY2006			X	
Iowa	FY2005			X	
Kansas	FY2005		X		
Kentucky	FY2005			X	
Maryland	FY2004	X			
Minnesota	FY2005	X			X
Mississippi	FY2005			X	
Missouri	FY2006	X			
New Jersey	FY2005			X	X
New York	FY2004		X		X
Rhode Island	FY2003	X			X
Texas	FY2006		X		
West Virginia	FY2005		X		

Source: Centers for Medicare and Medicaid Services. Report on the Health Insurance Flexibility and Accountability (HIFA) Initiative: State Accessibility to Funding for Coverage Expansions, Oct. 4, 2001; and Center on Budget and Policy Priorities. OMB Estimates Indicate That 900,000 Children Will Lose Health Insurance Due to Reductions in Federal SCHIP Funding, Aug. 2, 2002.

LEGISLATIVE ACTIVITY IN THE 108TH CONGRESS

Several bills have been introduced in the 108th Congress to modify the rules for redistribution and extended availability of SCHIP allotments. Ultimately H.R. 2854, a bill to amend title XXI of the Social Security Act to extend the availability of allotments for fiscal years 1998 through 2001 under the State Children's Health Insurance Program, was passed by the Congress and signed into law as P.L. 108-74 on August 15, 2003. P.L. 108-74 represents a bi-partisan compromise to reconcile differences among the earlier bills passed by the House and Senate (i.e., S. 312, and H.R. 531) during the 108th Congress. Detailed descriptions of the provisions included in each of the bills are described below.

SCHIP Financing Issues

The Senate passed a bill, S. 312, to amend Title XXI of the Social Security Act to extend the availability of allotments for fiscal years 1998 through 2001 under SCHIP, on June 26, 2003. S. 312 addresses many of the above-mentioned concerns by extending the availability of FY1998 and FY1999 reallocated funds through the end of FY2004 and establishing a new method for redistributing unspent allotments for FY2000 and for FY2001 for both those states spending all of their allotments and those that had not. This new method is a modified version of the special redistribution rules for unspent FY1998 and FY1999 allotments.

For each of FY2000 and FY2001, no more than 50% of the total amount of unspent funds would be available for redistribution to states, commonwealths, and territories that exhausted their SCHIP allotments for each of those years by the applicable 3-year deadline.[29] Subject to this ceiling, each such state would receive an amount equal to: 50% of the total amount of unspent funds for each of those years less amounts redistributed to the territories, all multiplied by the ratio of such state's excess spending, to total excess spending for all such states. Each territory would receive an amount equal to 1.05% of the total amount available for redistribution for each of those years multiplied by that territory's proportion of the original allotment available for all territories. The bill would make redistributed funds from the FY2000 reallocation available through the end of FY2004. Redistributed funds from the reallocations for FY2001 would be available through the end of fiscal year 2005.

For each of FY2000 and FY2001, the amount available for retention among those states that *did not* fully expend their SCHIP allotments by the applicable 3-year deadline would be equal to 50% of such state's unspent funds for each of those years. The bill would make retained funds for such jurisdictions from the FY2000 reallocation available through the end of FY2004. Retained funds from the reallocation for FY2001 would be available through the end of FY2005.

Similar to current law for FY1998 and FY1999, to calculate the amounts available for reallocation for FY2000 and FY2001, the Secretary would use expenditures reported by states not later than November 30 of the applicable calendar year.

---

[29] The purpose of the limits applied to the redistributions for FY2000 and FY2001 is to ensure that all states have access to at least some of the funds available for redistribution. This redistribution design would help states to sustain spending through the 3-year dip in appropriations.

In addition to the redistribution formula, S. 312 would allow "qualifying states" to use up to 20% of their original SCHIP allotment or their reallocated funds (for that fiscal year) in each of FY1998, FY1999, FY2000 and FY2001, for medical assistance payments under the state's regular Medicaid program associated with the coverage of children through age18 with family incomes greater than 150% FPL. Subject to availability of their SCHIP allotment or reallocated funds for the year, qualifying states would be eligible to receive an amount equal to the additional amount that would have been paid to such state for coverage of such children if such claims were matched at the state's Enhanced FMAP as opposed to the state's regular FMAP. Use of these funds for expenditures incurred under an approved Section 1115 waiver in the qualifying state would not impact the budget neutrality agreement for such states.[30] For example, when determining if a waiver meets the budget neutrality test, these savings may not be counted as an offset to ensure that the predicted "with waiver"costs do not exceed the "without waiver" costs as required by the budget neutrality agreement.

For a given fiscal year, "qualifying states" under S. 312 would include those which: (1) as of April 15, 1997, or under a Section 1115 waiver implemented on January 1, 1994, had a Medicaid income eligibility standard for at least one category of children (excluding infants) of at least 185% FPL; and (2) as of January 1, 2001 had a SCHIP eligibility standard of at least 200% FPL, or greater than 200% FPL if under a Section 1115 waiver targeted at uninsured children; (3) did not impose waiting lists or enrollment caps for children whose family income is at least 200% FPL; (4) provide statewide SCHIP coverage to all children who meet such state's income and other eligibility requirements; and (5) have implemented at least three of the following procedures for establishing children's eligibility for their Medicaid and SCHIP programs: (a) use the same uniform, simplified application form; (b) do not apply asset tests; (c) adopt 12-month continuous enrollment; (d) use the same forms, verification policies, and frequency for initial eligibility determinations and eligibility redeterminations; and/or (e) have procedures in place for initial eligibility determinations that can be made by disproportionate share hospital (DSH) facilities as well as federally qualified health centers.

---

[30] In 1994 the Clinton Administration published a notice in the *Federal Register* which describes the budget neutrality requirement for Section 1115 waivers. In this context, budget neutrality means that estimated spending under the waiver cannot exceed the estimated cost of the state's existing Medicaid program.

SCHIP Financing Issues

On June 26, 2003, the House passed H.R. 531, a bill to amend Title XXI of the Social Security Act to extend the availability of allotments for fiscal years 1998 through 2001 under the SCHIP. This bill is identical to S. 312 except that it does not include the provision that would allow "qualifying states" to use up to 20% of their original SCHIP allotment or their reallocated funds (for that fiscal year) for certain Medicaid medical assistance payments.

In the most recent legislative development regarding SCHIP financing, the House passed a new version of the bill, H.R. 2854, to restore the unspent FY1998 and FY1999 reallocated SCHIP funds in the same manner as described in S. 312, to establish a method for redistributing unspent allotments for FY2000 and for FY2001 for all states according to the same method described in S. 312, and to allow qualifying states to use up to 20% of their available SCHIP funds for certain Medicaid payments. In contrast to S. 312, under H.R. 2854, qualifying states would include those which on *and after*[31] April 15, 1997, had a Medicaid income eligibility standard for at least one category of children (excluding infants) of at least 185% FPL. The bill also identifies the Section 1115 waiver programs operating in Minnesota and Tennessee as those that would meet the definition of "qualifying states." All of the other additional qualifications listed in S. 312 were dropped. H.R. 2854, also includes a technical correction to the temporary increase of the Medicaid FMAP provision included in the Jobs and Growth Tax Relief Reconciliation Act of 2003 (P.L. 108-27).[32]

The Senate passed H.R. 2854 on July 31, 2003.[33] CBO cost estimates project that H.R. 2854 would increase direct spending in the SCHIP program by about $1.7 billion and would reduce Medicaid outlays by $795 million over the period FY2003- FY2007.[34] The bill was presented to the President

---

[31] Such states would be required to maintain their April 15, 1997 level of coverage (i.e., at least 185% FPL for one or more categories of children other than infants) to continue to meet the qualifying state criteria.

[32] For more information on the temporary increase of the Medicaid FMAP provisions included in the Jobs and Growth Tax Relief Reconciliation Act of 2003 (P.L. 108-27), see CRS Report RS21262, *Federal Medical Assistance Percentage (FMAP) for Medicaid* by Christine Scott.

[33] S. 1503 was introduced and referred to the Senate Committee on Finance on July 30, 2003. This bill has generated interest because it makes a technical correction to the definition of qualifying state as specified in H.R. 2854. If enacted, this bill would ensure that states with an income eligibility standard for one or more categories of children other than infants that is just under 185% (e.g., $184.5%) would also meet the definition of qualifying state.

[34] CBO's cost estimate for H.R. 2854 is available on their website at the following address [ftp://ftp.cbo.gov/44xx/doc4486/hr2854.pdf]

for his signature on August 7, 2003 and signed into law as P.L. 108-74 on August 15, 2003.

CONCLUSION

The availability of SCHIP allotments under current funding rules influences program design and planning. Unlike Medicaid, which operates as an individual entitlement, SCHIP operates as a capped grant program. Allotment of funds among states is determined by a formula set in law. Once a state depletes a given year's original allotment, other than funds from prior year(s) made available through redistribution, no additional federal funds will be made available to that state for that year. States have the flexibility under SCHIP statute to design their programs to operate within these funding constraints.

The allotment and redistribution methods under current law have not matched up with state spending patterns to date. Spending in the first several years of the program was well below appropriations — expenditure data through the end of FY2002 show that states spent approximately 46.9% of all available federal funds, leaving an unspent balance of approximately $10.7 billion from the FY1998 through FY2002 allotments. Relative to state spending, the appropriation levels were high early on as it took time for states to set up their programs and build enrollment. Once programs are established, states have shown a wide variability in the extent to which they utilize their allotments, with some states spending significantly less than their original allotments and some states spending more.

FY2002 is the first fiscal year in which total spending exceeded that year's appropriations. This trend is likely to continue as additional states spend all of their available funds and are eligible for redistributions. Further, FY2002 is the first of 3 years in which the total federal appropriation is 26% less than it was for each of FY1998-FY2001 and $1.3 billion of the BIPA-2000 reallocations as well as additional sums (approximately $1.4 billion) from the FY2000 redistributions are expected to expire from the program. While more states will be eligible for redistributions, there will be fewer funds available for redistribution to such states. In fact, CMS projects shortfalls for some states over the second half of the program (FY2003-FY2006).

SCHIP financing issues are being addressed by the 108th Congress because states with unspent funds from the FY1998 and FY1999 reallocations are interested in recouping those amounts and want to make sure that other unspent amounts from subsequent years remain available to their programs. Both the Senate and the House have passed H.R. 2854, a bill that attempts to strike a balance between policies to reward fast spending states with the underlying program tenet that SCHIP is a capped grant program under which states must design their programs carefully to stay within the budgetary limitations of their allotments. Under H.R. 2854, among other provisions, a new SCHIP redistribution formula is created that will allow unspent funds from the FY2000 and FY2001 allotments to remain available to all states for one additional year. Fifty percent of the unspent funds for each year will be distributed among states and territories that spent their entire allotment for a given year, and the remaining 50% of unspent funds will be retained and distributed among states that have not used their entire allotments. The bill was presented to the President for his signature on August 7, 2003 and signed into law as P.L. 108-74 on August 15, 2003.

APPENDIX 1. SHARE OF ORIGINAL FY1998, FY1999, AND FY2000 ALLOTMENTS EXPENDED BY DEADLINES (IN 000S)

State	FY1998			FY1999			FY2000		
	Original allotment	Expended	%	Original allotment	Expended	%	Original allotment	Expended	%
Alabama	$85,975	$57,311	66.7%	$85,569	$23,136	27.0%	$77,012	$28,819	37.0%
Alaska	$6,889	$6,889	100.0%	$6,857	$6,857	100.0%	$7,730	$7,730	100.0%
Arizona	$116,798	$38,242	32.7%	$116,246	$0	0.0%	$130,213	$75,293	58.0%
Arkansas	$47,908	$2,203	4.6%	$47,682	$0	0.0%	$53,754	$0	0.0%
California	$854,645	$257,012	30.1%	$850,609	$0	0.0%	$765,548	$23,061	3.0%
Colorado	$41,791	$23,943	57.3%	$41,593	$9,416	22.6%	$46,890	$17,691	38.0%
Connecticut	$34,959	$25,063	71.7%	$34,794	$6,788	19.5%	$39,225	$4,427	11.0%
Delaware	$8,053	$2,290	28.4%	$8,015	$0	0.0%	$9,036	$0	0.0%
District of Columbia	$12,076	$6,262	51.9%	$12,019	$1,522	12.7%	$10,817	$1,069	10.0%
Florida	$270,215	$183,046	67.7%	$268,939	$138,923	51.7%	$242,045	$215,487	89.0%
Georgia	$124,660	$56,178	45.1%	$124,071	$32,850	26.5%	$132,381	$67,637	51.0%
Hawaii	$8,945	$420	4.7%	$8,903	$0	0.0%	$10,037	$0	0.0%
Idaho	$15,880	$12,776	80.5%	$15,805	$10,982	69.5%	$17,818	$12,328	69.0%
Illinois	$122,529	$53,472	43.6%	$121,950	$0	0.0%	$137,481	$0	0.0%
Indiana	$70,512	$70,512	100.0%	$70,179	$70,170	100.0%	$63,161	$50,187	79.0%
Iowa	$32,460	$26,332	81.1%	$32,307	$20,889	64.7%	$32,383	$23,938	74.0%
Kansas	$30,657	$21,562	70.3%	$30,512	$18,735	61.4%	$30,321	$30,321	100.0%[c]
Kentucky	$49,933	$49,933	100.0%	$49,697	$49,697	100.0%	$56,026	$56,026	100.0%
Louisiana	$101,737	$35,655	35.0%	$101,256	$0	0.0%	$91,131	$19,653	22.0%
Maine	$12,487	$12,487	100.0%	$12,428	$12,428	100.0%	$13,978	$13,978	100.0%
Maryland	$61,627	$61,627	100.0%	$61,336	$61,336	100.0%	$56,870	$56,870	100.0%
Massachusetts	$42,836	$42,836	100.0%	$42,634	$42,634	100.0%	$48,064	$48,064	100.0%

State	FY1998			FY1999			FY2000		
	Original allotment	Expended	%	Original allotment	Expended	%	Original allotment	Expended	%
Michigan	$91,586	$51,727	56.5%	$91,153	$11,772	12.9%	$102,762	$6,299	6.0%
Minnesota	$28,396	$15	0.1%	$28,262	$0	0.0%	$31,861	$31,861	100.0%[c]
Mississippi	$56,017	$29,178	52.1%	$55,753	$31,665	56.8%	$58,036	$58,036	100.0%[c]
Missouri	$51,673	$51,673	100.0%	$51,429	$51,429	100.0%	$57,979	$1,278	2.0%
Montana	$11,740	$4,887	41.6%	$11,685	$9,430	80.7%	$13,173	$11,150	85.0%
Nebraska	$14,863	$9,881	66.5%	$14,793	$6,231	42.1%	$16,576	$8,219	50.0%
Nevada	$30,407	$13,064	43.0%	$30,263	$3,281	10.8%	$30,526	$9120	30.0%
New Hampshire	$11,458	$2,539	22.2%	$11,404	$0	0.0%	$10,264	$0	0.0%
New Jersey	$88,418	$70,008	79.2%	$88,000	$88,000	100.0%[b]	$96,859	$96,859	100.0%
New Mexico	$62,973	$4,210	6.7%	$62,675	$0	0.0%	$56,408	$0	0.0%
New York	$255,626	$255,626	100.0%	$254,419	$254,419	100.0%	$286,822	$286,822	100.0%
North Carolina	$79,508	$79,508	100.0%	$79,133	$79,133	100.0%	$89,211	$77,769	87.0%
North Dakota	$5,041	$1,859	36.9%	$5,017	$425	8.5%	$5,656	$1,900	34.0%
Ohio	$115,734	$97,580	84.3%	$115,188	$88,430	76.8%	$129,858	$117,815	91.0%
Oklahoma	$85,699	$51,257	59.8%	$85,294	$3,660	4.3%	$76,765	$0	0.0%
Oregon	$39,122	$20,148	51.5%	$38,937	$2,539	6.5%	$43,896	$1,026	2.0%
Pennsylvania	$117,457	$117,457	100.0%	$114,685	$96,243	83.9%	$121,063	$90,688	75.0%
Rhode Island	$10,684	$10,684	100.0%	$10,634	$10,634	100.0%	$9,571	$9,571	100.0%
South Carolina	$63,558	$63,558	100.0%	$63,258	$63,258	100.0%	$71,314	$71,314	100.0%
South Dakota	$8,541	$4,655	54.5%	$8,501	$2,720	32.0%	$7,951	$6,234	78.0%
Tennessee	$66,153	$41,705	63.0%	$65,841	$0	0.0%	$74,226	$0	0.0%
Texas	$561,332	$81,262	14.5%	$558,681	$0	0.0%	$502,812	$255,484	51.0%
Utah	$24,241	$20,836	86.0%	$24,127	$20,359	84.4%	$27,199	$24,259	89.0%
Vermont	$3,535	$1,955	55.3%	$3,519	$1,319	37.5%	$3,967	$1,631	41.0%
Virginia	$68,315	$23,550	34.5%	$67,992	$16	0.0%	$73,580	$11,234	15.0%
Washington	$46,661	$604	1.3%	$46,441	$0	0.0%	$52,355	$0	0.0%

State	FY1998			FY1999			FY2000		
	Original allotment	Expended	%	Original allotment	Expended	%	Original allotment	Expended	%
West Virginia	$23,607	$10,771	45.6%	$23,495	$13,907	59.2%	$21,146	$21,146	100.0%[c]
Wisconsin	$40,633	$23,461	57.7%	$40,441	$40,441	100.0%[b]	$45,592	$45,591	100.0%
Wyoming	$7,712	$1,041	13.5%	$7,675	$0	0.0%	$7,069	$0	0.0%
Total Five Territories	$10,738	$10,738	100.0%	$42,688	$42,688	100.0%	$44,888	$44,888	100.0%
MOE[a]	—	—	—	$2,217	$0	0.0%	$7,894	$0	0.0
Total	$4,235,000	$2,201,492	52.0%	$4,247,000	$1,428,373	33.6%	$4,249,200	$2,042,760	48.0%

Source: *Federal Register*, vol. 66, no. 120, June 21, 2001: p. 33263 and *Federal Register*, vol. 67, no. 81, Apr. 26, 2002, p. 20799, and Centers for Medicare and Medicaid Services, preliminary 4th quarter FY2002 state-reported expenditure data as of Nov. 30, 2002.

Note: Shaded cells represent states that spent all of their allotment by the applicable 3-year deadline, and thus qualified for redistributions of unspent funds (from other states).

[a] MOE refers to one of the maintenance of effort provisions in SCHIP statute. When SCHIP was created, three states — Florida, New York and Pennsylvania — had existing comprehensive state-based health benefit programs for children that were deemed to meet SCHIP requirements. These states are required to maintain their prior level of spending under SCHIP. Specifically, beginning in FY1999, the allotment for a given fiscal year will be reduced by the difference between the state's spending in the prior fiscal year versus fiscal year 1996 (before SCHIP began). The $7.9 million shown for MOE in this table reflects spending patterns in Pennsylvania for FY1999, in which Pennsylvania's share of SCHIP costs was $7.9 million less than FY1996 spending, so its allotment for FY2000 has been reduced by $7.9 million. This amount will be included in the redistribution process for FY2000. (Pennsylvania's share of FY1998 SCHIP costs was $2.2 million less than FY1996 spending, and its SCHIP allotment for FY1999 was reduced by $2.2 million. This amount is not shown in the MOE cell because it has already been redistributed to other states in the FY1999 redistribution process.)

[b] New Jersey and Wisconsin show an uncommon spending pattern for FY1998 and FY1999. Both states left a portion of FY1998 funds unspent at the 3-year deadline (end of FY2000). States are not permitted to access the succeeding year's allotment (in this case, FY1999 funds) until the prior year's allotment (in this case, FY1998 funds) is fully expended, or the deadline for availability of the prior year's funds has passed. Therefore these 2 states could not begin accessing their FY1999 allotments until FY2001, the final year of availability for FY1999 allotments. Despite their not having spent all of the FY1998 allotment by the 3-year deadline, both states spent their entire FY1999 allotments in FY2001, and thus qualified for redistributions of unspent FY1999 funds (from other states) which were made available during FY2002.

[c] Kansas, Minnesota, Mississippi, and West Virginia show an uncommon spending pattern for FY1999 and FY2000. Each of these states left a portion of FY1999 funds unspent at the 3-year deadline (end of FY2001). States are not permitted to access the succeeding year's allotment (in this case, FY2000 funds) until the prior year's allotment (in this case, FY1999 funds) is fully expended, or the deadline for availability of the prior year's funds has passed. Therefore these 4 states could not begin accessing their FY2000 allotments until FY2002, the final year of availability for FY2000 allotments. Despite their not having spent all of the FY1998 allotment by the 3-year deadline, or their FY1999 allotment by the 3-year deadline these states spent their entire FY2000 allotments in FY2002, and thus will qualified for redistributions of unspent FY2000 funds (from other states) which will be made available during FY2003.

APPENDIX 2. SHARE OF FY1998 AND FY1999 BIPA-2000 REALLOCATIONS EXPENDED BY DEADLINE AND INTERIM FY2000 REALLOCATION PAYMENT AMOUNTS FOR UNEXPENDED FY2000 SCHIP ALLOTMENTS (IN 000S)

State	FY1998 reallocations			FY1999 reallocations			FY2000 interim reallocation payment amounts
	Redistributed/ retained allotment	Expended	%	Redistributed/ retained allotment	Expended	%	Interim redistributed allotment
Alabama	$18,512	$18,512	100.0%	$26,175	$26,175	100.0%	
Alaska	$15,006	$15,006	100.0%	$38,614	$21,014	54.4%	$20,231
Arizona	$50,733	$50,733	100.0%	$48,736	$48,736	100.0%	
Arkansas	$29,518	$4,011	13.6%	$19,990	-	0.0%	
California	$385,970	$385,970	100.0%	$356,616	$356,616	100.0%	
Colorado	$11,527	$11,527	100.0%	$13,490	$13,490	100.0%	
Connecticut	$6,391	$6,391	100.0%	$11,741	$11,741	100.0%	
Delaware	$3,722	$3,722	100.0%	$3,360	$1,178	35.0%	
District of Columbia	$3,755	$3,755	100.0%	$4,401	$4,401	100.0%	
Florida	$56,296	$56,296	100.0%	$54,509	$54,509	100.0%	
Georgia	$44,228	$44,228	100.0%	$38,245	$38,245	100.0%	
Hawaii	$5,506	$5,506	100.0%	$3,733	$1,437	38.5%	
Idaho	$2,005	$2,005	100.0%	$2,022	$2,022	100.0%	
Illinois	$44,599	$44,599	100.0%	$51,127	$30,825	60.3%	
Indiana	$44,908	$44,908	100.0%	$105,203	-	0.0%	
Iowa	$3,958	$3,958	100.0%	$4,787	$4,787	100.0%	
Kansas	$5,874	$5,874	100.0%	$4,937	$4,937	100.0%	$21,481

State	FY1998 reallocations			FY1999 reallocations				FY2000 interim reallocation payment amounts
	Redistributed/ retained allotment	Expended	%	Redistributed / retained allotment	Expended	%		Interim redistributed allotment
Kentucky	$27,919	$27,919	100.0%	$96,297	$34,340	35.7%		$71,982
Louisiana	$42,678	$42,678	100.0%	$42,452	$42,452	100.0%		
Maine	$4,532	$4,532	100.0%	$18,728	$5,532	29.5%		$14,670
Maryland	$44,657	$44,657	100.0%	$137,136	$93,872	68.5%		$114,946
Massachusetts	$36,715	$36,715	100.0%	$87,173	$19,468	22.3%		$53,097
Michigan	$25,742	$25,742	100.0%	$33,280	$33,280	100.0%		
Minnesota	$18,329	$18,329	100.0%	$11,849	$11,849	100.0%		$16,766
Mississippi	$17,333	$17,333	100.0%	$10,099	$10,099	100.0%		$40,864
Missouri	$9,236	$9,236	100.0%	$61,787	$61,787	100.0%		
Montana	$4,426	$4,426	100.0%	$945	$945	100.0%		
Nebraska	$3,217	$3,217	100.0%	$3,589	$3,589	100.0%		
Nevada	$11,201	$11,201	100.0%	$11,312	$11,312	100.0%		
New Hampshire	$5,760	$5,760	100.0%	$4,781	$1,113	23.3%		
New Jersey	$11,889	$11,889	100.0%	$107,350	$107,350	100.0%		$110,932
New Mexico	$37,951	$21,918	57.8%	$26,277	-	0.0%		
New York	$434,890	$434,890	100.0%	$729,772	$174,076	23.9%		$414,465
North Carolina	$20,902	$20,902	100.0%	$92,147	-	0.0%		
North Dakota	$2,055	$2,055	100.0%	$1,925	$1,925	100.0%		
Ohio	$11,725	$11,725	100.0%	$11,218	$11,218	100.0%		
Oklahoma	$22,244	$22,244	100.0%	$34,225	$30,157	88.1%		
Oregon	$12,254	$12,254	100.0%	$15,260	$15,260	100.0%		
Pennsylvania	$5,590	$5,590	100.0%	$7,732	$7,732	100.0%		
Rhode Island	$1,987	$1,987	100.0%	$20,381	$20,381	100.0%		$25,048

	FY1998 reallocations			FY1999 reallocations			FY2000 interim reallocation payment amounts
State	Redistributed/ retained allotment	Expended	%	Redistributed/ retained allotment	Expended	%	Interim redistributed allotment
South Carolina	$52,514	$8,009	15.3%	$75,055	-	0.0%	$32,649
South Dakota	$2,510	$2,510	100.0%	$2,424	$2,424	100.0%	
Tennessee	$15,789	$15,789	100.0%	$27,604	$2,645	9.6%	
Texas	$310,044	$310,044	100.0%	$234,226	$234,226	100.0%	
Utah	$2,199	$2,199	100.0%	$1,579	$1,579	100.0%	
Vermont	$1,021	$1,021	100.0%	$922	$922	100.0%	
Virginia	$28,911	$28,911	100.0%	$28,499	$28,499	100.0%	
Washington	$29,745	$13,576	45.6%	$19,470	-	0.0%	
West Virginia	$8,290	$8,290	100.0%	$4,020	$4,020	100.0%	$18,804
Wisconsin	$11,090	$11,090	100.0%	$38,614	$38,416	100.0%	$55,796
Wyoming	$4,308	$4,308	100.0%	$3,218	$1,811	56.3%	
Total Five	$21,352	$21,352	100.0%	$29,596	$28,826	97.4%	$23,168
Total	$2,033,508	$1,931,294	95.0%	$2,818,627	$1,661,415	58.9%	$1,034,899

Source: Centers for Medicare and Medicaid Services, preliminary 4th quarter FY2002 state-reported expenditure data as of Nov. 30, 2002 and Centers for Medicare and Medicaid Services (CMS) Letter to State Medicaid Directors and State Health Officials (SMDL #03-003), Mar. 27, 2003.

Note: Shaded cells represent states with remaining BIPA-2000 reallocations at the close of FY2002. Cells containing "-" represent states that did not access reallocated funds during the period of availability. CMS permitted states to access reallocated funds from FY1998 during FY2001 and FY2002, and reallocated funds from FY1999 during FY2002. These reallocated funds became additional active accounts whose availability overlapped with other original allotments (at which point remaining funds reverted to the Treasury). On Mar. 27, 2003, CMS published an interim policy for a partial redistribution of unexpended FY2000 allotments (available for redistribution after Sept. 30, 2002). The interim redistribution was limited to approximately one-half of the unexpended FY2000 allotments ($1.03 billion) and was targeted to states, commonwealths, and territories that fully spent such allotments by the end of FY2002. These amounts appear in the last column of this table.

Chapter 2

MEDICARE PROVISIONS IN THE MEDICARE, MEDICAID, AND SCHIP BENEFITS IMPROVEMENT AND PROTECTION ACT OF 2000 (BIPA, P.L. 106-554)[*]

Hinda Ripps Chaikind, Sibyl Tilson, Jennifer O'Sullivan, Carolyn Merck and Madeleine Smith

BACKGROUND

Since the passage of the Balanced Budget Act of 1997 (BBA, P.L. 105-33) Medicare spending has set records for low or declining rates of program growth. In fiscal year 1998, the Medicare growth rate slowed to a then record low of just 1.5% for the entire year, an amount less than would be expected allowing for increases in enrollment and for inflation. The following year set a new record, when, for the first time in the program's history Medicare spending dropped from one year to the next. Mandatory program spending declined by about $2 billion, from $211 billion in 1998 to

---

[*] Excerpted from CRS Report RL30707.

$209.3 billion in 1999, almost a 1% decline. According to the Department of the Treasury, Medicare spending for 2000 increased by about 3%.

Although part of the slower rates of growth may be attributed to underestimates of the savings derived from the BBA, it is difficult to pinpoint any one factor as the exact cause for this projected decline in spending. Many factors other than the BBA, such as an improved economic forecast and heightened anti-fraud activities, are significant components of the decline in the rates of growth in Medicare spending.

Provider groups argue that the BBA reductions have threatened both their economic viability and their ability to provide services for Medicare beneficiaries. However, government studies have indicated that this lower rate of growth has not resulted in inadequate reimbursement rates. For example, reports on the Medicare+Choice (M+C) program by both the Department of Health and Human Services (HHS) and the GAO indicate that payment levels are not too low. The Inspector General of the HHS reported in September, 2000 that M+C organizations "receive more than an adequate amount of funds to deliver the Medicare package of covered services". GAO also reported in August, 2000 on their examination of 1998 payments, the second year that plans were paid using the M+C payment rates. Their examination showed that the M+C program spent about $3.2 billion or over 13% more on health plan enrollees than if these enrollees had received services through traditional fee-for-service Medicare. Despite these findings, M+C organizations are withdrawing from the program; disrupting coverage to many Medicare beneficiaries.

Studies of the adequacy of payment extend beyond the M+C program. The Inspector General of HHS, in a series of reports on skilled nursing facilities (SNFs), reported that even under the new prospective payment system, most hospital discharge planners were able to place patients that need care in a nursing facility.

Congress first addressed the issue of slower rates of growth in Medicare spending with the passage of the Balanced Budget Refinement Act of 1999 (BBRA, P.L. 106-113). At time of passage, CBO estimated that the BBRA would add approximately $16 billion in total back into the Medicare program for 2001-2005.

CBO's July 2000 estimates of Medicare spending, released in July, 2000 projected that Medicare spending growth over the course of the 2001 to 2010 decade would average 7.3% annually. Over that period, Medicare's share of the U.S. national income was projected to increase from 2.3% of Gross Domestic Product (GDP) in 2000 to 2.8% by 2010. Most of Medicare's program growth was expected to result from two factors: increased enrollment and automatic updates in reimbursements for services.

The table below compares CBO's July 2000 projections with two earlier estimates: those made in July 1999, just prior to the passage of the BBRA, and the January, 1997, estimates calculated prior to the passage of the BBA. As shown in the table, according to CBO's July 2000 projections, Medicare would spend about a total of $1.339 trillion over the following 5 years (2001-2005). These figures reflected the downward trend in estimates. For the 5-year period, CBO's estimated spending was lower by $60 billion, a 4% reduction. Concurrently, the projected rate of growth for Medicare spending for the 5-year period was reduced from 7.8% per year to 7.5% per year. Comparing the July 2000 estimates to pre-BBA estimates, computed 3 years ago, showed a significant decline in the projected rate of growth. Five-year estimates of Medicare spending were down by $378 billion, or more than 20%, with a concomitant decline in the estimated average annual rate of growth from 9.4% to 7.5% per year.

Table 1. CBO Baseline Estimates for Medicare
(fiscal year, dollars in billions)

	5 years (2001-2005)
Mandatory Outlays	
CBO Pre-BBA Baseline	(1/97) $1,717
CBO Pre-BBRA Baseline	(7/99) $1,399
CBO July 2000 Baseline (7/00)	$1,339
Change	
Pre-BBA to Pre-BBRA Baseline	-$318
Pre-BBRA to July 2000 Baseline	-$60
Total Change	-$378
Average Annual Rates of Growth	
CBO Pre-BBA Baseline (1/97)	9.4%
CBO Pre-BBRA Baseline (7/99)	7.8%
CBO July 2000 Baseline (7/00)	7.5%

Source: U.S. Congressional Budget Office.
Notes:
1) Mandatory Outlays include benefits outlays and only mandatory administration outlays. It does not include discretionary administration outlays.
2) BBA is the Balanced Budget Act of 1997.
3) BBRA is the Balanced Budget Refinement Act of 1999.

LEGISLATION IN 2ND SESSION OF THE 106TH CONGRESS

Budget Resolution

The 106th Congress debated and then passed legislation that would increase funding to the Medicare program. The FY2001 Budget Resolution (H.Con.Res. 290) earmarked specific funds for the Medicare spending. The conference report (H.Rept. 106-577, approved by both House and Senate on April 13, 2000) contained assumptions of both the House and Senate bills. In the House, there was a $40 billion reserve fund over 5 years (2001-2005) for legislation to provide for Medicare reform and prescription drug coverage. In the Senate, there was a two-part reserve fund. The first part was a 5-year $20 billion fund for legislation to provide for prescription drugs. The second part was a $40 billion reserve fund for legislation improving the solvency of Medicare and improving access to prescription drugs (or continuing access provided under the first part). Funds available under the second part would be reduced by any amounts made available under the first part. The $40 billion figure was close to the 5-year cost estimate for the drug benefit included in the Administration's original bill. The CBO estimate for the Administration's revised proposal was higher ($98.5 billion over the FY2001-FY2005 period.)

Medicare Bills

The House Commerce Committee[1] ordered reported H.R.5291 (*Beneficiary Improvement and Protection Act of 2000*) on September 27, 2000 and the Ways and Means Subcommittee on Health ordered reported its bill to the full committee October 3, 2000. (The House Ways and Means Committee has jurisdiction over Part A of the Medicare program, the Hospital Insurance program, and shares jurisdiction with the House Commerce Committee over Part B, the Supplementary Medical Insurance program.) Each of these bills provided additional funding to the Medicare program. Senator Roth of the Senate Finance Committee introduced S.3165, on October 5, 2000, a bill which also increased Medicare program funding.

---

[1] The House Commerce Committee has been renamed the House Energy and Commerce Committee in the 107th Congress.

(In the Senate, the Senate Finance Committee has sole jurisdiction over Medicare, i.e., over both Part A and Part B of the program.)

Based on the provisions in the House Ways and Means, House Commerce, and Senate Finance Committee legislation, these three committees, together with House and Senate leadership, proposed an agreement, the Medicare, Medicaid, and SCHIP Benefits Improvement and Protection Act of 2000. This agreement was attached to H.R. 2614 and passed by the House of Representatives on October 26, 2000. On December 14, 2000, Representative Thomas introduced H.R. 5661, which included the Medicare (as well as Medicaid, SCHIP and other) provisions of H.R. 2614, with a few modifications. On December 15, 2000, the House and the Senate passed H.R. 4577, the Consolidated Appropriations Act of 2001, which incorporated by reference H.R. 5661. The Medicare legislative proposals included in H.R. 5661 were designed to increase payments for many of the services covered by the Medicare program, such as hospitals, Medicare+Choice organizations, home health agencies, and skilled nursing facilities. The legislation also included limited expansions of certain preventive benefits and modified the appeals and coverage processes, but did not address the issue of prescription drug coverage.

CBO estimates that this legislation will increase Medicare spending by $32.3 billion over the 5-year period (2001-2005) and $81.5 billion over the 10-year period (2001-2010).[2] A substantial portion of these funds would be spent on the Medicare+Choice program; $11.2 billion over 5 years and $32.5 billion over 10 years. CBO also estimated a significant increase in federal spending for hospital outpatient services ($5.7 billion over 5 years and $14.2 billion over 10 years) and hospital inpatient services ($5.2 billion over 5 years and $9.6 billion over 10 years). The remainder of the spending increase would be spread across Medicare to cover beneficiary improvements, rural health care, skilled nursing facilities, hospice care, physicians and other Medicare services. The total federal budgetary impact on the Medicare, Medicaid, and SCHIP programs is projected to be $17 billion over 5 years and $15.1 billion over 10 years. These spending estimates reflect the increased Medicare spending which is significantly offset by savings to the Medicaid program. However, this report is limited to describing the Medicare proposals included in the bill.

---

[2] CBO estimate, "Estimated Budgetary Effects of Medicare, Medicaid, and SCHIP Benefits Improvement and Protection of 2000 (H.R. 5661)."

MEDICARE PROVISIONS OF THE MEDICARE, MEDICAID, AND SCHIP BENEFITS IMPROVEMENT AND PROTECTION ACT OF 2000

Title I – Medicare Beneficiary Improvements

Subtitle A – Improved Preventive Benefits

Section 101. Coverage of Biennial Screening Pap Smear and Pelvic Exam

The provision modifies current law to provide Medicare coverage for biennial screening pap smears and pelvic exams, effective July 1, 2001.

Section 102. Coverage of Screening for Glaucoma.

The provision adds Medicare coverage for annual glaucoma screenings, beginning January 1, 2002, for persons determined to be at high risk for glaucoma, individuals with a family history of glaucoma, and individuals with diabetes. The service must be furnished by or under the supervision of an optometrist or ophthalmologist who is legally authorized to perform such services in the state where the services are furnished.

Section 103. Coverage of Screening Colonoscopy for Average Risk Individuals

The provision authorizes coverage for screening colonoscopies, beginning July 1, 2001, for all individuals, not just those at high risk. For persons not at high risk, payments cannot be made for such procedures if performed within 10 years of a previous screening colonoscopy or within 4 years of a screening flexible sigmoidoscopy.

Section 104. Modernization of Screening Mammography Benefit.

Beginning in 2002, the provision eliminates the statutorily prescribed payment rate for mammography payments and specifies that the services are to be paid under the physician fee schedule. The provision specifies two new payment rates for mammographies that utilize advanced new technology for the period April 1, 2001 to December 31, 2001. Payment for technologies that directly take digital images equal 150% of what would otherwise be paid for a bilateral diagnostic mammography. For technologies that convert standard film images to digital form, an additional payment of fifteen dollars is authorized. The Secretary is required to determine whether a new code is required for tests furnished after 2001.

Section 105. Coverage of Medical Nutrition Therapy Services for Beneficiaries with Diabetes or a Renal Disease

The provision establishes, effective January 1, 2002, Medicare coverage for medical nutrition therapy services for beneficiaries who have diabetes or a renal disease. Medical nutrition therapy services are defined as nutritional diagnostic, therapy and counseling services for the purpose of disease management which are furnished by a registered dietician or nutrition professional, pursuant to a referral by a physician. The provision specifies that the amount paid for medical nutrition therapy services equals the lesser of the actual charge for the service or 85% of the amount that would be paid under the physician fee schedule if such services were provided by a physician. Assignment is required for all claims. The Secretary is required to submit a report to Congress that contains an evaluation of the effectiveness of services furnished under this provision.

Subtitle B – Other Beneficiary Improvements

Section 111. Acceleration of Reduction of Beneficiary Copayment for Hospital Outpatient Department Services.

Effective April 1, 2001, the provision modifies current law by limiting the amount of a beneficiary's copayment for a procedure in a hospital outpatient department to the hospital inpatient deductible applicable in that year.

In addition, starting in April 2001, the provision requires the Secretary of HHS to reduce the effective copayment rate for outpatient services to a maximum rate of 57% and then gradually reduce the effective coinsurance rate in 5 percentage point intervals from 2002 through 2006 until the maximum rate is 40% in 2006. As stated in BBA 97, hospitals may waive any increase in coinsurance that may have arisen from the implementation of the outpatient prospective payment system (PPS).

The Comptroller General is required to work with the National Association of Insurance Commissioners (NAIC) to evaluate the extent to which premiums for supplemental policies reflect the acceleration of the reduction in beneficiary coinsurance for hospital outpatient services and result in savings to beneficiaries, and to report to the Congress by April 1, 2004.

Section 112. Preservation of Coverage of Drugs and Biologicals Under Part B of the Medicare Program

The provision clarifies policy with regard to coverage of drugs, provided incident to physicians services, that cannot be self-administered. The provision specifies that such drugs are covered when they are not usually self-administered by the patient.

Section 113. Elimination of Time Limitation on Medicare Benefits for Immunosuppressive Drugs

The provision eliminates the current time limitations on the coverage of immunosuppressive drugs for beneficiaries who have received a covered organ transplant. The provision applies to drugs furnished, on or after the date of enactment.

Section 114. Imposition of Billing Limits on Drugs

The provision specifies that payment for drugs under Part B must be made on the basis of assignment.

Section 115. Waiver of 24-Month Waiting Period for Medicare Coverage of Individuals Disabled with Amyotrophic Lateral Sclerosis (ALS)

The provision waives the 24-month waiting period (otherwise required for an individual to establish Medicare eligibility on the basis of a disability) for persons medically determined to have amyotrophic lateral sclerosis (ALS). The provision is effective July 1, 2001.

Subtitle C – Demonstration Projects and Studies

Section 121. Demonstration Project for Disease Management for Severely Chronically Ill Medicare Beneficiaries

The Secretary is required to conduct a demonstration project to illustrate the impact on costs and health outcomes of applying disease management to Medicare beneficiaries with diagnosed, advanced-stage congestive heart failure, diabetes, or coronary heart disease. Up to 30,000 beneficiaries may enroll, on a voluntary basis, for disease management services related to their chronic health condition. In addition, contractors providing disease management services are responsible for providing beneficiaries enrolled in the project with prescription drugs.

Section 122. Cancer Prevention and Treatment Demonstration for Ethnic and Racial Minorities

The provision requires the Secretary to conduct demonstration projects for the purpose of developing models and evaluating methods that improve the quality of cancer prevention services, improve clinical outcomes, eliminate disparities in the rate of preventive screening measures, and promote collaboration with community-based organizations for ethnic and racial minorities.

Section 123. Study on Medicare Coverage of Routine Thyroid Screening

The provision requires the Secretary to request the National Academy of Sciences, and as appropriate in conjunction with the United States Preventive Services Task Force, to analyze the addition of routine thyroid screening under Medicare. The analysis must consider the short term and long term benefits and cost to Medicare of adding such coverage for some or all beneficiaries.

Section 124. Medpac Study on Consumer Coalitions

The provision requires MedPAC to conduct a study that examines the use of consumer coalitions in the marketing of Medicare+Choice plans. A consumer coalition is defined as a non-profit community-based organization that provides information to beneficiaries about their health options under Medicare and negotiates with Medicare+Choice plans on benefits and premiums for beneficiaries who are members of the coalition or otherwise affiliated with it.

Section 125. Study on Limitation on State Payment for Medicare Cost-Sharing Affecting Access to Services for Qualified Medicare Beneficiaries

The provision requires the Secretary of HHS to conduct a study to determine if access to certain services (including mental health services) has been affected by a specific provision in law. That provision specifies that states are not required to pay Medicare cost-sharing charges for QMBs to the extent these payments would result in a total payment in excess of the Medicaid level.

Section 126. Studies on Preventive Interventions in Primary Care for Older Americans

The provision requires the Secretary, acting through the United States Preventive Services Task Force, to conduct a series of studies designed to identify preventive interventions in primary care for older Americans.

Section 127. Medpac Study and Report on Medicare Coverage of Cardiac and Pulmonary Rehabilitation and Therapy Services

The provision requires MedPAC to conduct a study on coverage of cardiac and pulmonary rehabilitation therapy services under Medicare.

Section 128. Lifestyle Modification Program Demonstration

The provision modifies the current Medicare demonstration project, known as the Lifestyle Modification Program. It extends the project to 4 years and assures that no fewer than 1,800 beneficiaries complete the entire course of treatment under the Program. The provision requires a study of its cost-effectiveness. An initial report is required within 1 year after 900 beneficiaries complete the Program and a final report is required within 1 year after 1,800 beneficiaries complete the Program.

Title II – Rural Health Care Improvements

Subtitle A – Critical Access Hospital Provisions

Section 201. Clarification of No Beneficiary Cost-Sharing for Clinical Diagnostic Laboratory Tests Furnished by Critical Access Hospitals

Effective for services furnished on or after the enactment of BBRA99, Medicare beneficiaries are not liable for any coinsurance, deductible, copayment, or other cost sharing amount with respect to clinical diagnostic laboratory services furnished as an outpatient critical access hospital (CAH) service. Conforming changes that clarify that CAHs are reimbursed on a reasonable cost basis for outpatient clinical diagnostic laboratory services are also included.

Section 202. Assistance with Fee Schedule Payment for Professional Services under All-Inclusive Rate

Effective for items and services furnished on or after July 1, 2001, Medicare will pay a CAH for outpatient services based on reasonable costs or, at the election of an entity, will pay the CAH a facility fee based on reasonable costs plus an amount based on 115% of Medicare's fee schedule for professional services.

Section 203. Exemption of Critical Access Hospital Swing Beds from SNF PPS

Swing beds in critical access hospitals (CAHs) are exempted from the SNF prospective payment system. CAHs are to be paid for covered SNF services on a reasonable cost basis.

Section 204. Payment in Critical Access Hospitals for Emergency Room on-Call Physicians

When determining the allowable, reasonable cost of outpatient CAH services, the Secretary must recognize amounts for the compensation and related costs for oncall emergency room physicians who are not present on the premises, are not otherwise furnishing services, and are not on-call at any other provider or facility. The Secretary must define the reasonable payment amounts and the meaning of the term "on-call." The provision is effective for cost reporting periods beginning on or after October 1, 2001.

Section 205. Treatment of Ambulance Services Furnished by Certain Critical Access Hospitals

Ambulance services provided by a critical access hospital (CAH) or provided by an entity that is owned or operated by a CAH will be paid on a reasonable cost basis if the CAH or entity is the only provider or supplier of ambulance services that is located within a 35-mile drive of the CAH. The provision is effective for cost reporting periods beginning on or after implementation of the fee schedule.

Section 206. GAO Study on Certain Eligibility Requirements for Critical Access Hospitals

Within 1 year of enactment, GAO is required to conduct a study on the eligibility requirements for critical access hospitals (CAHs) with respect to limitations on average length of stay and number of beds, including an analysis of the feasibility of having a distinct part unit as part of a CAH and the effect of seasonal variations in CAH eligibility requirements. GAO also is required to analyze the effect of seasonal variations in patient admissions on critical access hospital eligibility requirements with respect to limits on average annual length of stay and number of beds.

Subtitle B – Other Rural Hospitals Provisions

Section 211. Treatment of Rural Disproportionate Share Hospitals

For discharges occurring on or after April 1, 2001, all hospitals are eligible to receive DSH payments when their DSH percentage (threshold amount) exceeds 15%. The DSH payment formulas for sole community hospitals (SCHs), rural referral centers (RRCs), rural hospitals that are both SCHs and RRCs, small rural hospitals and urban hospitals with less than 100 beds are modified.

Section 212. Option to Base Eligibility for Medicare Dependent, Small Rural Hospital Program on Discharges During Two of the Three Most Recent Audited Cost Reporting Periods

An otherwise qualifying small rural hospital may be classified as an MDH if at least 60% of its days or discharges were attributable to Medicare Part A beneficiaries in at least two of the three most recent audited cost reporting periods for which the Secretary has a settled cost report.

Section 213. Extension of Option to Use Rebased Target Amounts to All Sole Community Hospitals

Any SCH may elect payment based on hospital specific, updated FY1996 costs if this target amount resulted in higher Medicare payments. A transition period is established with Medicare payment based completely on updated FY1996 hospital specific costs for discharges occurring after FY2003.

Section 214. Medpac Analysis of Impact of Volume on Per Unit Cost of Rural Hospitals with Psychiatric Units

MedPAC is required to report on the impact of volume on the per unit cost of rural hospitals with psychiatric units and include in its report a recommendation on whether special treatment is warranted.

Subtitle C – Other Rural Provisions

Section 221. Assistance for Providers of Ambulance Services in Rural Areas

The provision makes additional payments to providers of ground ambulance services for trips originating in rural areas that are greater than 17 miles and up to 50 miles. The payments are made for services furnished on or after July 1, 2001 and before January 1, 2004. The provision requires the Comptroller General to conduct a study to examine both the costs of efficiently providing ambulance services for trips originating in rural areas and the means by which rural areas with low population densities can be identified for the purpose of designating areas in which the costs of ambulance services would be expected to be higher. The Comptroller General must submit a report to Congress by June 30, 2002 on the results of the study, together with recommendations on steps that should be taken to assure access to ambulance services for trips originating in rural areas. The Secretary is required to take these findings into account when establishing the fee schedule, beginning with 2004.

Section 222. Payment for Certain Physician Assistant Services.

This provision gives permanent authority to physician assistants who owned rural health clinics which lost their designation as such to bill Medicare directly.

Section 223. Revision of Medicare Reimbursement for Telehealth Services

The provision establishes revised payment provisions, effective no later than October 1, 2001, for services that are provided via a telecommunications system by a physician or practitioner to an eligible beneficiary in a rural area. The Secretary is required to make payments for telehealth services to the physician or practitioner at the distant site in an amount equal to the amount that would have been paid to such physician or practitioner if the service had been furnished to the beneficiary without the use of a telecommunications system. A facility fee is paid to the originating site. Originating sites include a physician or practitioner office, a critical access hospital, a rural health clinic, a federally qualified health center, or a hospital. The Secretary is required to conduct a study, and submit recommendations to Congress, that identify additional settings, sites, practitioners and geographic areas that are appropriate for telehealth services. Entities participating in federal demonstration projects approved by, or receiving funding from, the Secretary as of December 31, 2000 are qualified sites.

Section 224. Expanding Access to Rural Health Clinics

All hospitals of less than 50 beds that own rural health clinics are exempt from the per-visit limit.

Section 225. Medpac Study on Low-Volume, Isolated Rural Health Providers

MedPAC is required to study the effect of low patient and procedure volume on the financial status and Medicare payment methods for hospital outpatient services, ambulance services, hospital inpatient services, skilled nursing facility services, and home health services in isolated rural health care providers.

Title III – Provisions Relating to Part A

Subtitle A – Inpatient Hospital Services

Section 301. Revision of Acute Care Hospital Payment Update for 2001

All hospitals will receive the full market basket index (MBI) as an update for FY2001. In order to implement this increase for hospitals other than sole community hospitals (SCH), those hospitals will receive the MBI minus 1.1 percentage points (the current statutory provision) for discharges occurring on or after October 1, 2000 and before April 1 2001; these non-SCH hospitals will receive the MBI plus 1.1 percentage points for discharges occurring on or after April 1, 2001 and before October 1, 2001. As indicated by Section 547(a), this payment increase does not apply to discharges occurring after FY2001. For FY2002 and FY2003, hospitals will receive the MBI minus .55 percentage points. For FY2004 and subsequently, hospitals will receive the MBI.

The Secretary is directed to consider the prices of blood and blood products purchased by hospitals in the next rebasing and revision of the hospital market basket to determine whether those prices are adequately reflected in the market basket index. MedPAC is directed to conduct a study on increased hospital costs attributable to complying with new blood safety measures and providing such services using new technologies among other issues.

For discharges occurring on or after October 1, 2001, the Secretary may adjust the standardized amount in future fiscal years to correct for changes in the aggregate Medicare payments caused by adjustments to the DRG weighting factors in a previous fiscal year (or estimates that such adjustments for a future fiscal year) that did not take into account coding improvements or changes in discharge classifications and did not accurately represent increases in the resource intensity of patients treated by PPS hospitals.

Section 302. Additional Modification in Transition for Indirect Medical Education (IME) Percentage Adjustment

Teaching hospitals will receive a 6.25% IME payment adjustment (for each 10% increase in teaching intensity) for discharges occurring on or after October 1, 2000 and before April 1, 2001. The IME adjustment will increase to 6.75% for discharges on or after April 1, 2001 and before October 1, 2001. As indicated in Section 547(a), the payment increase does not apply to discharges after FY2001. The IME adjustment is 6.5% in FY2002 and 5.5% in FY2003 and in subsequent years.

Section 303. Decrease in Reductions for Disproportionate Share Hospital (DSH) Payments

Reductions in the DSH payment formula amounts are 2% in FY2001, 3% in FY2002, and 0% in FY2003 and subsequently. To implement the FY2001 provision, DSH amounts for discharges occurring on or after October 1, 2000 and before April 1, 2001, are reduced by 3%, which was the reduction in effect prior to enactment of this provision. DSH amounts for discharges occurring on or after April 1, 2001 and before October 1, 2001 are reduced by only 1 percentage point. As indicated by Section 547(a), this payment adjustment does not apply to discharges after FY2001.

Section 304. Wage Index Improvements

For FY2001 or any fiscal year thereafter, a Medicare Geographic Classification Review Board (MGCRB) decision to reclassify a prospective payment system hospital for use of a different area's wage index is effective for 3 fiscal years. The Secretary must establish procedures whereby a hospital could elect to terminate this reclassification decision before the end of such period. For FY2003 and subsequently, MGCRB must base any comparison of the average hourly wage of the hospital with the average hourly wage for hospitals in the area using data from the each of the two immediately preceding surveys as well as data from the most recently published hospital wage survey.

The Secretary must establish a process which would first be available for discharges occurring on or after October 1, 2001 where a single wage index is computed for all geographic areas in the state. If the Secretary applies a statewide geographic index, an application by an individual hospital is not considered. The Secretary must also collect occupational data every 3 years in order to construct an occupational mix adjustment for the hospital area wage index. The first complete data collection effort must occur no later than September 30, 2003 for application beginning October 1, 2004.

Section 305. Payment for Inpatient Services in Rehabilitation Hospitals

Total payments for rehabilitation hospitals in FY2002 equals the amounts of payments that would have been made if the rehabilitation prospective payment system (PPS) had not been enacted. A rehabilitation facility may make a one-time election before the start of the PPS to be paid based on a fully phased-in PPS rate.

Section 306. Payment for Inpatient Services of Psychiatric Hospitals

The provision increases the incentive payments for psychiatric hospitals and distinct part units to 3% for cost reporting periods beginning on or after October 1, 2000.

Section 307. Payment for Inpatient Services of Long-Term Care Hospitals

For cost reporting periods beginning during FY2001, the national cap for long term hospitals is increased by 2% and the target amount is increased by 25%. Neither these payments nor the increased bonus payments provided by BBRA 99 may be factored into the development of the prospective payment system (PPS) for long term hospitals. When developing the PPS for inpatient long term hospitals, the Secretary is required to examine the feasibility and impact of basing payment on the existing (or refined) acute hospital DRGs and using the most recently available hospital discharge data. If the Secretary is unable to implement a long term hospital PPS by October

1, 2002, the Secretary is required to implement a PPS for these hospitals using the existing acute hospital DRGs that have been modified where feasible.

Subtitle B – Adjustments to PPS Payments for Skilled Nursing Facilities

Section 311. Elimination of Reduction in Skilled Nursing Facility (SNF) Market Basket Update in 2001

The provision modifies the schedule and rates according to which federal per diem payments are updated. In FY2002 and FY2003 the updates are the market basket index increase minus 0.5 percentage point. The update rate for the period October 1, 2000, through March 31, 2001, is the market basket index increase minus 1 percentage point; the update rate for the period April 1, 2001, through September 30, 2001, is the market basket index increase plus one percentage point (this increase must not be included when determining payment rates for the subsequent period). Temporary increases in the federal per diem rates provided by BBRA 99 are in addition to the increases in this provision. By July 1, 2002, the Comptroller General is required to submit a report to Congress on the adequacy of Medicare payments to SNFs, taking into account the role of private payers, Medicaid, and case mix on the financial performance of SNFs and including an analysis, by RUG classification, of the number and characteristics of such facilities. By January 1, 2005, the Secretary is required to submit a report to Congress on alternatives for classification of SNF patients.

Section 312. Increase in Nursing Component of PPS Federal Rate

The provision increases the nursing component of each RUG by 16.66% over current law for SNF care furnished after April 1, 2001, and before October 1, 2002. The Comptroller General is required to conduct an audit of nurse staffing ratios in a sample of SNFs and to report to Congress by August 1, 2002, on the results of the audit of nurse staffing ratios and recommend whether the additional 16.66% payment should be continued.

Section 313. Application of SNF Consolidated Billing Requirement Limited to Part a Covered Stays

Effective January 1, 2001, the provision limits the current consolidated billing requirement to services and items furnished to SNF residents in a Medicare Part A covered stay and to therapy services furnished in Part A and

Part B covered stays. The Inspector General of HHS is required to monitor Part B payments to SNFs on behalf of residents who are not in a Part A covered stay.

Section 314. Adjustment of Rehabilitation RUGS to Correct Anomaly in Payment Rates

Effective for skilled nursing facility (SNF) services furnished on or after April 1, 2002, the provision increases by 6.7% certain federal per diem payments to ensure that Medicare payments for SNF residents with "ultra high" and "high" rehabilitation therapy needs are appropriate in relation to payments for residents needing "medium" or "low" levels of therapy. The 20% additional payment that was provided in BBRA 99 for certain RUGS is removed to make this provision budget neutral.

The Inspector General of HHS is required to review and report to Congress by October 1, 2001, regarding whether the RUG payment structure as in effect under the BBRA 99 includes incentives for the delivery of inadequate care.

Section 315. Establishment of Process for Geographic Reclassification

The provision permits the Secretary to establish a process for geographic reclassification of skilled nursing facilities based upon the method used for inpatient hospitals. The Secretary may implement the process upon completion of the data collection necessary to calculate an area wage index for workers in skilled nursing facilities.

Subtitle C – Hospice Care

Section 321. Five Percent Increase in Payment Base

The provision increases Medicare daily payment rates for hospice care furnished on or after April 1, 2001, and during FY2001 by 5 percentage points over the rates in effect in FY2000. For determining payment rates for FY2002, the 5 percentage point increase shall be considered in the FY2001 rates. The temporary increase in payment rates provided in BBRA 99 for FY2001 and FY2002 (.5% and .75%, respectively) shall be included in the base on which updates are computed.

Section 322. Clarification of Physician Certification

Effective for certifications of terminal illness made on or after the date of enactment, the provision modifies current law to specify that the physician's or hospice medical director's certification of terminal illness is based on his/her clinical judgment regarding the normal course of the individual's illness. The Secretary is required to study and report to Congress within 2 years of enactment on the appropriateness of certification of terminally ill individuals and the effect of this provision on such certification.

Section 323. Medpac Report on Access to, and Use of, Hospice Benefit

The provision requires MedPAC to examine the factors affecting the use of Medicare hospice benefits, including delay of entry into the hospice program and urban and rural differences in utilization rates. The provision requires a report on the study to be submitted to Congress 18 months after enactment.

Subtitle D – Other Provisions

Section 331. Relief from Medicare Part A Late Enrollment Penalty for Group Buy-in for State and Local Retirees

The provision exempts certain state and local retirees, retiring prior to January 1, 2002, from the Part A delayed enrollment penalties. These would be groups of persons for whom the state or local government elected to pay the delayed Part A enrollment penalty for life. The amount of the delayed enrollment penalty which would otherwise be assessed is reduced by an amount equal to the total amount of Medicare payroll taxes paid by the employee and the employer on behalf of the employee. The provision applies to premiums for months beginning with January 1, 2002.

Title IV – Provisions Relating to Part B

Subtitle A – Hospital Outpatient Services

Section 401. Revision of Hospital Outpatient PPS Payment Update

The provision modifies the current law update rates applicable to the hospital outpatient PPS by providing in FY2001 an update equal to the full rate of increase in the market basket index. As under current law, the increase in FY2002 would be the market basket index increase minus one percentage point.

A special rule applies to the OPD PPS rates in 2001: For the period January 2, 2001, through March 31, 2001, the PPS amounts shall be those in effect on the day before implementation of the new law. For the periods April 1, 2001, through December 31, 2001, the PPS amounts in effect during the prior period shall be increased by 0.32%.

Effective as if enacted with BBA 97, if the Secretary determines that updates to the adjustment factor used to convert the relative utilization weights under the PPS into payment amounts have, or are likely to, result in hospitals' changing their coding or classification of covered services, thereby changing aggregate payments, the Secretary is authorized to adjust the conversion factor in later years to eliminate the effect of coding or classification changes.

Section 402. Clarifying Process and Standards for Determining Eligibility of Devices for Pass-through Payments under Hospital Outpatient PPS

The provision modifies the procedures and standards by which certain medical devices are categorized and determined eligible for pass-through payments under the PPS. Through public rule-making procedures, the Secretary is required to establish criteria for defining special payment categories under the PPS for new medical devices. The Secretary must promulgate, through the use of a program memorandum, initial categories that would encompass each of the individual devices that the Secretary had designated as qualifying for the pass-through payments to date. In addition, similar devices not so designated because they were payable under Medicare prior to December 31, 1996, also must be included in initial categories. The Secretary is required to create additional new categories in the future to accommodate new technologies meeting the "not insignificant cost" test established in BBRA 99.

Once the categories are established, pass-through payments currently authorized under Section 1833(t)(b) of the Social Security Act will proceed on a categoryspecific, rather than device-specific basis. These payments are designated as "category-based pass-through payments." These payments will continue to be made for the 2 to 3 years payment period originally specified in BBRA 99, and, for each given category, will begin when the first such payment is made for any device included in a specified category. At the conclusion of this transitional payment period, categories will sunset and payment for the device will be included in the underlying PPS payment for the related service.

Section 403. Application of OPD PPS Transitional Corridor Payments to Certain Hospitals that Did Not Submit a 1996 Cost Report

Effective as if enacted with BBRA 99, the provision modifies current law as enacted in BBA 99 to enable all hospitals, not just those hospitals filing 1996 cost reports, to be eligible for transitional payments under the PPS.

Section 404. Application of Rules for Determining Provider-Based Status for Certain Entities

The provision grandfathers existing arrangements whereby certain entities (such as outpatient clinics, skilled nursing facilities, etc.) are considered "provider-based" entities, meaning they are affiliated financially and clinically with a main hospital. Existing provider-based status designations continue for 2 years beginning October 1, 2000. If a facility or organization requests approval for provider-based status during the period October 1, 2000, through September 30, 2002, it shall be treated as if it had such status during the period of time the determination is pending. In making such a status determination on or after October 1, 2000, HCFA shall treat the applicant as satisfying any requirements or standards for geographic location if it satisfied geographic location requirements in regulations or is located not more than 35 miles from the main campus of the hospital.

An applicant facility or organization is treated as satisfying all requirements for provider-based status if it is owned or operated by a unit of state or local government or is a public or private nonprofit corporation that is formally granted governmental powers by a unit of state or local government, or is a private hospital that, under contract, serves certain low income households or has a certain disproportionate share adjustment.

These provisions are in effect during a 2-year period beginning on October 1, 2000.

Section 405. Treatment of Children's Hospitals under Prospective Payment System

The BBRA 99 provides special "hold harmless" payments to ensure that cancer hospitals would receive no less under the hospital outpatient PPS than they would have received, in aggregate, under the "pre-BBA" system, that is, the pre-PPS payment system. Effective as if included in the BBRA 99, the provision extends this hold harmless protection to children's hospitals.

Section 406. Inclusion of Temperature Monitored Cryoablation in Transitional Pass-Through for Certain Medical Devices, Drugs, and Biologicals under OPD PPS

The provision includes temperature monitored cryoablation as part of the transitional pass-through for certain medical devices, drugs, and biologicals under the hospital outpatient prospective payment system, effective April 1, 2001.

Subtitle B – Provisions Relating to Physicians Services

Section 411. GAO Studies Relating to Physicians Services

The provision requires the GAO to conduct a study on the appropriateness of furnishing in physicians' offices specialist services (such as gastrointestinal endoscopic physicians services) which are ordinarily furnished in hospital outpatient departments. The GAO also must study the refinements to the practice expense relative value units made during the transition to the resource-based system.

Section 412. Physician Group Practice Demonstration

The provision requires the Secretary to conduct demonstration projects to test, and if proven effective, expand the use of incentives to health care groups participating under Medicare. Such incentives must be designed to encourage coordination of care furnished under Medicare Parts A and B by institutional and other providers and practitioners; to encourage investment in administrative structures and processes to encourage efficient service delivery; and to reward physicians for improving health outcomes. The Secretary must establish, for each group participating in a demonstration, a base expenditure amount and an expenditure target (reflecting base expenditures adjusted for risk and expected growth rates). The Secretary will pay each group a bonus for each year equal to a portion of the savings for the year relative to the target. In addition, at such time as the Secretary has developed appropriate criteria, the Secretary will pay an additional bonus related to process and outcome improvements. Total payments under demonstrations must not exceed what the Secretary estimates would be paid in the absence of the demonstration program.

Section 413. Study on Enrollment Procedures for Groups that Retain Independent Contractor Physicians.

The provision requires the Comptroller General to conduct a study of the current Medicare enrollment process for groups that retain independent contractor physicians; particular emphasis is placed on hospital-based physicians, such as emergency department staffing groups.

Subtitle C – Other Services

Section 421. One-Year Extension of Moratorium on Therapy Caps; Report on Standards for Supervision of Physical Therapy Assistants

The provision extends the moratorium on the physical therapy and occupational therapy caps for 1 year through 2002; it also extends the requirement for focused reviews of therapy claims for the same period. The Secretary is required to conduct a study on the implications of eliminating the "in the room" supervision requirement for Medicare payment for physical therapy assistants who are supervised by physical therapists and the implications of this requirement on the physical therapy cap.

Section 422. Updatei In Renal Dialysis Composite Rate

The provision increases the composite rate payment for renal dialysis services by 2.4% for 2001. The provision requires the Secretary to collect data and develop an end-stage renal disease (ESRD) market basket whereby the Secretary can estimate, before the beginning of a year, the percentage increase in costs for the mix of labor and non-labor goods and services included in the composite rate. The Secretary shall report to Congress on the index together with recommendations on the appropriateness of an annual or periodic update mechanism for dialysis services. The Comptroller General must study the access of beneficiaries to dialysis services. There is a hold harmless provision for facilities who received exceptions for their 2000 rates. In addition, facilities that did not apply for an exception in 2000 may apply in the first 6 months of 2001. The exceptions rates would remain in effect so long as the rate is greater than the updated composite rate. The provision would specify that for the period January 1, 2001-March 31, 2001, the applicable composite rate is the rate in effect before enactment of this provision. The rate in effect for the period April 1, 2001-December 31, 2001, is the rate established under this section increased by a transitional percentage allowance equal to 0.39%.

Section 423. Payment for Ambulance Services

The provision provides for the full inflation update in ambulance payments for 2001. It also specifies that any phase-in of the ambulance fee schedule must provide for full payment of national mileage rates in states where separate mileage payments were not made prior to implementation of the fee schedule. The provision specifies that for the period January 1, 2001-June 30, 2001, the inflation update is that determined prior to enactment of this provision. For services furnished from July 1, 2001-December 31, 2001, the update is 4.7%. The provision relating to mileage payments is effective July 1, 2001.

Section 424. Ambulatory Surgical Centers

The provision delays implementation of proposed regulatory changes to the ambulatory payment classification system, which are based on 1994 cost data, until January 1, 2002. At that time, such changes will be phased in over 4 years: in the first year the payment amounts will be 25% of the revised rates and 75% of the prior system rates; in the second year payments will be 50% of the revised rates and 50% of the prior system rates, etc. The provision also requires that the revised system, based on 1999 (or later) cost data, be implemented January 1, 2003. (The phase-in of the revised system and 1994 data ends when the system with 1999 or later data is implemented.)

Section 425. Full Update for Durable Medical Equipment

The provision would modify updates to payments for durable medical equipment. For 2001, the payments for covered DME are increased by the full increase in the consumer price index for urban consumers (CPI-U) during the 12-month period ending June 2000. In general, in 2002 and thereafter, the annual update equals the full increase in the CPI-U for the 12 months ending the previous June. The provision specifies that for the period January 1, 2001, through June 30, 2000, the applicable amounts paid for DME are the amounts in effect before enactment of this provision. The amounts in effect for the period July 1, 2001, through December 31, 2001, are the amounts established under this section increased by a transitional allowance of 3.28%.

Section 426. Full Update for Orthotics and Prosthetics

The provision modifies updates to payments for orthotics and prosthetics. In 2000, the rates are increased by 1%. In 2001, the increase equals the percentage increase in the CPI-U during the 12-month period ending with June, 2000. For 2002, payments are increased by 1% over the prior year's amounts. The provision specifies that for the period January 1, 2001, through June 30, 2001, the applicable amounts paid for these items are the amounts in effect before enactment of this provision. The amounts in effect for the period July 1, 2001, through December 31, 2001, are the amounts established under this section increased by a transitional allowance of 2.6%.

Section 427. Establishment of Special Payment Provisions and Requirements for Prosthetics and Certain Custom Fabricated Orthotic Items

Under the provision, certain prosthetics or custom fabricated orthotics are covered by Medicare if furnished by a qualified practitioner and fabricated by a qualified practitioner or qualified supplier. The Secretary must establish a list of such items in consultation with experts. Within 1 year of enactment, the Secretary must promulgate regulations to provide these items, using negotiated rulemaking procedures.

Not later than 6 months from enactment, the Comptroller General must submit to Congress a report on the Secretary's compliance with the Administrative Procedures Act with regard to HCFA Ruling 96-1; certain impacts of that ruling; the potential for fraud and abuse in provision of prosthetics and orthotics under special payment rules and for custom fabricated items; and the effect on Medicare and Medicaid payments if that ruling were overturned.

Section 428. Replacement of Prosthetic Devices and Parts

The provision authorizes Medicare coverage for replacement of artificial limbs, or replacement parts for such devices, if ordered by a physician for specified reasons. Effective for items furnished on or after enactment, coverage applies to prosthetic items 3 or more years old, and supersedes any 5-year age rules for such items under current law.

Section 429. Revised Part B Payment for Drugs and Biologicals and Related Services

The provision requires the Comptroller General to study and submit a report to Congress and the Secretary on the reimbursement for drugs and biologicals and for related services under Medicare; the report must include specific recommendations for revised payment methodologies. The Secretary must revise the current payment methodologies for covered drugs and biologicals and related services based on these recommendations; however, total payments under the revised methodologies may not exceed the aggregate payments the Secretary estimates would have been made under the current law. The provision establishes a moratorium on changes in payment rates, in effect on January 1, 2001, until the Secretary reviews the GAO report.

Section 430. Contrast Enhanced Diagnostic Procedures under Hospital Prospective Payment System

The provision requires the Secretary to create under the hospital outpatient PPS additional and separate groups of covered services which include procedures that utilize contrast media. The provision applies to items and services furnished on or after January 1, 2002. The provision adds contrast agents to the medical devices, drugs, and biologicals for which additional payments are provided above and beyond the hospital outpatient department PPS amount, effective July 1, 2001.

Section 431. Qualifications for Community Mental Health Centers

The provision clarifies the qualifications for community mental health centers providing partial hospitalization services under Medicare.

Section 432. Payment of Physician and Nonphysician Services in Certain Indian Providers

The provision authorizes hospitals and free-standing ambulatory care clinics of the Indian Health Service or operated by a tribe or tribal organization to bill Medicare Part B for certain services furnished at the direction of the hospital or clinic. Services covered under the provision are those furnished under the physician fee schedule and services furnished by a practitioner or therapist under a fee schedule. The provision is effective July 1, 2001.

Section 433. GAO Study on Coverage of Surgical First Assisting Services of Certified Registered Nurse First Assistants

The provision requires the Comptroller General to conduct a study on the effect on both the program and beneficiaries of covering surgical first assisting services of certified registered nurse first assistants.

Section 434. Medpac Study and Report on Medicare Reimbursement for Services Provided by Certain Providers

The provision requires MedPAC to conduct a study on the appropriateness of current payment rates for services provided by a certified nurse midwife, physician assistant, nurse practitioner, and clinical nurse specialist.

Section 435. Medpac Study and Report on Medicare Coverage of Services Provided by Certain Non-Physician Providers

The provision requires MedPAC to conduct a study to determine the appropriateness of Medicare coverage of the services provided by a surgical technologist, marriage counselor, pastoral care counselor, and licensed professional counselor of mental health.

Section 436. GAO Study and Report on the Costs of Emergency And Medical Transportation Services

The provision requires the Comptroller General to conduct a study on the costs of providing emergency and medical transportation services across the range of acuity levels of conditions for which such transportation services are provided.

Section 437. GAO Studies and Reports on Medicare Payments

The provision requires the Comptroller General to conduct a study on the postpayment audit process for physicians services, including the proper level of resources HCFA should devote to educating physicians regarding coding and billing, documentation requirements, and calculation of overpayments. The Comptroller General is also required to conduct a study of the aggregate effects of regulatory, audit, oversight and paperwork burdens on physicians and other health care providers participating in Medicare.

Section 438. Medpac Study on Access to Outpatient Pain Management Services

The provision requires MedPAC to conduct a study on the barriers to coverage and payment for outpatient interventional pain medicine procedures under Medicare.

Title V – Provision Relating to Parts A and B

Subtitle A – Home Health Services

Section 501. One-Year Additional Delay in Application of 15% Reduction on Payment Limits for Home Health Services

The provision requires that the aggregate amount of Medicare payments to home health agencies in the second year of the PPS (FY2002) shall equal the aggregate payments in the first year of the PPS, updated by the market basket index (MBI) increase minus 1.1 percentage points. The 15% reduction to aggregate PPS amounts, which, under current law, would go into effect October 1, 2001, are delayed until October 1, 2002. The Comptroller General (rather than the Secretary) must submit, by April 1, 2002, a report analyzing the need for the 15% or other reduction. If the Secretary determines that updates to the PPS system for a previous fiscal year (or estimates of such adjustments for a future fiscal year) did (or are likely to) result in a change in aggregate payments due to changes in coding or classification of beneficiaries' service needs that do not reflect real changes in case mix, effective for home health episodes concluding on or after October 1, 2001, the Secretary may adjust PPS amounts to eliminate the effect of such coding or classification changes.

Section 502. Restoration of Full Home Health Market Basket Update for Home Health Services for FY2001

The provision modifies the home health PPS updates. During the period October 1, 2000, through March 31, 2001, the rates promulgated in the home health PPS regulations on July 3, 2000, apply for 60-day episodes of care (or visits) ending in that period. For the period April 1, 2001, through September 31, 2001, those rates are increased by 2.2% for 60-day episodes (or visits) ending in that time period. This increase is included in determining subsequent payment amounts.

Section 503. Temporary 2-Month Extension of Periodic Interim Payments

The provision extends, for certain home health agencies, applicability of periodic interim payments provided under current law. Home health agencies that were receiving such payments as of September 30, 2000, will continue to receive them until December 1, 2000. The payment is a one-time payment equal to 4 times the last 2- week payment the agency received before implementation of the home health PPS on October 1, 2000. The amounts are included in the agency's last settled cost report before implementation of the PPS.

Section 504. Use of Telehealth in Delivery of Home Health Services

The provision clarifies that the telecommunications provisions should not be construed as preventing a home health agency from providing a service, for which payment is made under the prospective payment system, via a telecommunications system, provided that the services do not substitute for "in-person" home health services ordered by a physician as part of a plan of care, or are not considered a home health visit for purposes of eligibility or payment.

Section 505. Study on Costs to Home Health Agencies of Purchasing Nonroutine Medical Supplies

The provision requires that, not later than October 1, 2001, the Comptroller General shall submit to Congress a report regarding the variation in prices home health agencies pay for nonroutine supplies, the volume of supplies used, and what effect the variations have on the provision of services. The Secretary is required to make recommendations on whether Medicare payment for those supplies should be made separately from the home health PPS.

Section 506. Treatment of Branch Offices; GAO Study on Supervision of Home Health Care Provided in Isolated Rural Areas

The provision clarifies that neither time nor distance between a home health agency parent office and a branch office shall be the sole determinant of a home health agency's branch office status. The Secretary is authorized to include forms of technology in determining "supervision" for purposes of determining a home health agency's branch office status.

Not later than January 1, 2002, the Comptroller General must submit to Congress a report regarding the adequacy of supervision and quality of home health services provided by home health agency branch offices and subunits in isolated rural areas, and to make recommendations on whether national standards for supervision would be appropriate in assuring quality.

Section 507. Clarification of the Homebound Definition Under the Medicare Home Health Benefit

The provision specifies that beneficiaries may not be disqualified for home health care as a result of their leaving home if they use adult day care in a licensed facility for therapeutic, psychosocial, or medical treatment purposes. The provision also clarifies that homebound beneficiaries may attend religious services without being disqualified from Medicare coverage for home health care.

Section 508. Temporary Increase for Home Health Services Furnished in a Rural Area

For home health services furnished in certain rural areas from April 1, 2001, through September 31, 2002, Medicare payments are increased by 10%, without regard to budget neutrality for the overall home health prospective payment system. This temporary increase is not included in determining subsequent payments.

Subtitle B – Direct Graduate Medical Education

Section 511. Increase in Floor for Direct Graduate Medical Education Payments

A hospital's approved per resident amount for cost reporting periods beginning during FY2002 are not less than 85% of the locality adjusted national average per resident amount.

Section 512. Change in Distribution Formula for Medicare+Choice-Related Nursing and Allied Health Education Costs

A hospital will receive nursing and allied health payments for Medicare managed care enrollees based on its per day cost of allied and nursing health programs and number of days attributed to Medicare enrollees in comparison to that in all other hospitals. The provision is effective for portions of cost reporting periods occurring on or after January 1, 2001.

Subtitle C – Changes in Medicare Coverage and Appeals Process

Section 521. Revisions to Medicare Appeals Process

The provision modifies the Medicare appeals process. Generally, initial determinations by the Secretary shall be concluded no later than 45-days from the date the Secretary received a claim for benefits. Any individual dissatisfied with the initial determination is entitled to a redetermination by the carrier or fiscal intermediary who made the initial determination. Such redetermination must be completed within 30 days of a beneficiary's request. Beneficiaries may appeal the outcome of a redetermination by seeking a reconsideration. Generally, a request for a reconsideration must be initiated no later than 180 days after the date the individual receives the notice of an adverse redetermination. In addition, if contested amounts are greater than $100, an individual may appeal an adverse reconsideration decision by requesting a hearing by the Secretary (first for a hearing by an administrative law judge, then in certain circumstances, for a hearing before the Department Appeals Board). If the dispute is not satisfactorily resolved through this administrative process, and if contested amounts are greater than $1,000, the individual may request judicial review of the Secretary's final decision. Aggregation of claims to meet these thresholds are permitted.

An expedited determination is available for a beneficiary who received notice: 1) that a provider plans to terminate services and a physician certifies that failure to continue the provisions of the services is likely to place the beneficiary's health at risk; or 2) that the provider plans to discharge the beneficiary.

The Secretary shall enter into 3-year contracts with at least 12 qualified independent contractors (QICs) to conduct reconsiderations. A QIC must promptly notify beneficiaries and Medicare claims processing contractors of its determinations. A beneficiary may appeal the decision of a QIC to an ALJ. In cases where the ALJ decision is not rendered within the 90-day deadline, the appealing party may request a DAB hearing.

The Secretary shall perform outreach activities to inform beneficiaries, providers, and suppliers of their appeal rights and procedures. The Secretary must submit to Congress an annual report including information on the number of appeals for the previous year, identifying issues that require administrative or legislative actions, and including recommendations for change as necessary. The report must also contain an analysis of the consistency of the QIC determinations as well as the cause for any identified inconsistencies.

Section 522. Revisions to Medicare Coverage Process

The provision clarifies when and under what circumstances Medicare coverage policy may be challenged. An aggrieved party may file a complaint concerning a national coverage decision. Such complaint is reviewed by the Department Appeals Board (DAB) of HHS. The provision also permits an aggrieved party to file a complaint concerning a local coverage determination. In this case, the determination is reviewed by an administrative law judge. If unsatisfied, complainants may subsequently seek review of such a local policy by the DAB. In both cases, a DAB decision constitutes final HHS action, and is subject to judicial review. The Secretary is required to implement DAB decisions and ALJ decisions (in the case of a local coverage policy) within 30 days. The provision also permits an affected party to submit a request to the Secretary to issue a national coverage or noncoverage determination if one has not been issued. The Secretary has 90 days to respond. HHS is required to prepare an annual report on national coverage determinations.

Subtitle D – Improving Access to New Technologies

Section 531. Reimbursement Improvements for New Clinical Laboratory Tests and Durable Medical Equipment

The provision specifies that the national limitation amount for a new clinical laboratory test would equal 100% of the national median for such test. The Secretary is required to establish procedures that permit public consultation for coding and payment determinations for new clinical diagnostic laboratory tests and new durable medical equipment. The Secretary must report to Congress on specific procedures used to adjust payments for advanced technologies; the report must include recommendations for legislative changes needed to assure fair and appropriate payments.

Section 532. Retention of HCPCS Level III Codes

The provision extends the time for the use of local codes (known as HCPCS level III codes) through December 31, 2003; the Secretary is required to make the codes available to the public.

Section 533. Recognition of New Medical Technologies Under Medicare Inpatient Hospital PPS

The Secretary must submit a report to Congress no later than April 1, 2001, on potential methods for more rapidly incorporating new medical services and technologies used in the inpatient setting in the clinical coding system used with respect to payment for inpatient services. The Secretary must identify the preferred methods for expediting these coding modifications in his report, and to implement such method by October 1,

2001. Additional hospital payments could be made by means of a new technology group (DRG), an add-on payment, payment adjustment or other mechanism. However, separate fee schedules for additional new technology payments are not permitted. The Secretary must implement the new mechanism on a budget neutral basis. The total amount of projected additional payments under the mechanism is limited to an amount not greater than the Secretary's annual estimation of the costs attributable to the introduction of new technology in the hospital sector as a whole (as estimated for purposes of the annual hospital update calculation).

Subtitle E – Other Provisions

Section 541. Increase in Reimbursement for Bad Debt

Effective beginning with cost reports starting in FY2001, the provision increases the percentage of the reasonable costs associated with beneficiaries' bad debt in hospitals that Medicare would reimburse to 70.

Section 542. Treatment of Certain Physician Pathology Services Under Medicare

The provision permits independent laboratories under a grandfather arrangement to continue, for a 2-year period (2001-2002), direct billing for the technical component of pathology services provided to hospital inpatients and hospital outpatients. The Comptroller General is required to conduct a study of the effect of these provisions on hospitals and laboratories and access of fee-for-service beneficiaries to the technical component of physician pathology services. The report is to include recommendations on whether the provisions should continue after the 2-year period for either (or both) inpatient and outpatient hospital services and whether the provision should be extended to other hospitals.

Section 543. Extension of Advisory Opinion Authority

The Office of the Inspector General's authority to issue advisory opinions to outside parties who request guidance on the applicability of the anti-kickback statute, safe harbor provisions, and other OIG health care fraud and abuse sanctions is made permanent.

Section 544. Change in Annual Medpac Reporting

The provision delays the reporting date for the MedPAC report on issues affecting the Medicare program by 15 days to June 15. The provision also requires record votes on recommendations contained both in this report and the March report on payment policies.

Section 545. Development of Patient Assessment Instruments

The provision requires the Secretary to report to the Congress on the development of standard instruments for the assessment of the health and functional status of patients and make recommendations on the use of such standard instruments for payment purposes.

Section 546. GAO Report on Impact of the Emergency Medical Treatment and Active Labor Act (EMTALA) on Hospital Emergency Departments

GAO must evaluate the impact of the Emergency Medical Treatment and Active Labor Act on hospitals, emergency physicians, and on-call physicians covering emergency departments and to submit a report to Congress by May 1, 2001.

Section 547. Clarification of Application of Temporary Payment Increases for 2001

The special increases and adjustments of the acute hospital payment update, the indirect medical education adjustment, and the disproportionate share hospital adjustment that are in effect between April and October 2001 do not apply to discharges after FY2001 and are not included in determining subsequent payments.

Special update payments under the skilled nursing facility prospective payment system between April and October 2001 do not apply to SNF services furnished after that period and are not included when determining payments for the subsequent period.

Special market basket update payments under the home health prospective payment system between April and October 2001 are not included in determining subsequent payments. Also, temporary payments to certain rural home health agencies from April 1, 2001, through September 30, 2002, are not included in determining subsequent payments.

Title VI – Provisions Relating to Part C Medicare+Choice Program) and Other Medicare Managed Care Provisions

Subtitle A – Medicare+Choice Payment Reforms

Section 601. Increase in Minimum Payment Amount

The provision sets the minimum payment amount for aged enrollees *within* the 50 states and the District of Columbia in a Metropolitan Statistical Area with a population of more than 250,000 at $525 in 2001. For all other areas *within* the 50 states and the District of Columbia, the minimum is $475. For any area *outside* the 50 states and the District of Columbia, the $525 and $475 minimum amounts are also applied, except that the 2001 minimum payment amount cannot exceed 120% of the 2000 minimum payment amount. This increase is effective March 1, 2001.

Section 602. Increase in Minimum Percentage Increase

This provision applies a 3% minimum update in 2001 and return to the current law minimum update of 2% thereafter. This increase is effective March 1, 2001.

Section 603. Phase-in of Risk Adjustment

This provision extends the current risk adjustment methodology until 2003, under which 10% of payments are based on risk-adjusted inpatient data built on the 15 principal inpatient diagnostic cost groups (PIP-DCGs) and 90% are adjusted solely using the older demographic method. Beginning in 2004, a new risk adjustment methodology will be phased-in based on data from inpatient hospitals and ambulatory settings. This new risk adjustment will be phased in at the rate of 30% in 2004, 50% in 2005, and 75% in 2006. Beginning in 2007, risk adjustment will be based entirely on data from inpatient hospitals and ambulatory settings.

Section 604. Transition to Revised Medicare+Choice Payment Rates

Within 2 weeks after the date of enactment of the Act, the Secretary announced revised M+C capitation rates for 2001 (completed on January 4, 2001), due to changes from this Act. Plans that previously provided notice of their intention to terminate contracts or reduce their service area for 2001 have 2 weeks after announcement of the revised rates (January 18, 2001) to rescind their notice and submit ACR information. Further, any M+C organization that will receive higher capitation payments as a result of this Act must submit revised ACR information within 2 weeks after announcement of the revised rates. Plans may only reduce premiums, reduce cost sharing, enhance benefits, utilize stabilization funds, or stabilize or enhance beneficiary access to providers (as long as this does not result in increased beneficiary premiums, increased cost-sharing, or reduced benefits). Any regulations that limit stabilization fund amounts will be waived, with respect to ACR submissions under this section of the bill. Notwithstanding the issuance of revised rates, M+C organizations will continue to be paid on a fee-for-service basis for costs associated with new national coverage determinations that are made mid-year.

Section 605. Revision of Payment Rates for ESRD Patients Enrolled in Medicare+Choice Plans

This provision requires that the Secretary increase the M+C payment rates for enrollees with ESRD. The revised rates will reflect the demonstration rate (including the risk-adjustment methodology) of social health maintenance organizations' ESRD capitation demonstrations. The revised rates will include adjustments for factors such as renal treatment modality, age, and underlying cause of the disease. These revised rates will be effective beginning in January 2002, and the Secretary of HHS is required to publish the adjustments in final form by July 1, 2001.

Section 606. Permitting Premium Reductions as Additional Benefits Under Medicare+Choice Plans

This provision permits M+C plans to offer reduced Medicare Part B premiums to their enrollees as part of providing any required additional benefits or reduced costsharing. An M+C organization may elect a reduction in its M+C payment up to 125% of the annual Part B premium. However, only 80% of this amount can be used to reduce an enrollee's actual Part B premium. This has the effect of returning up to 100% of the beneficiary's Part B premium. The reduction applies uniformly to each enrollee of the M+C plan. Plans must include information about Part B premium reductions as part of the required information that is provided to enrollees for comparing plan options. This provision will be effective beginning in 2003.

Section 607. Full Implementation of Risk Adjustment for Congestive Heart Failure Enrollees For 2001

This provision fully implements risk adjustment based on inpatient hospital diagnoses for an individual who had a qualifying congestive heart failure inpatient diagnosis between July 1, 1999 and June 30, 2000, if that individual was enrolled in a coordinated care plan offered on January 1, 2001. This will apply for only 1 year, beginning on January 1, 2001. This payment amount will be excluded from the determination of the budget neutrality factor.

Section 608. Expansion of Application of Medicare+Choice New Entry Bonus

This provision expands the application of the new entry bonus for M+C plans to include areas for which notification had been provided, as of October 3, 2000, that no plans are available January 1, 2001.

Section 609. Report on Inclusion of Certain Costs of the Department of Veterans Affairs and Military Facility Services in Calculating Medicare+Choice Payment Rates

The Secretary shall report to Congress by January 1, 2003, on a method to phase-in the costs of military facility services furnished by the Department of Veterans Affairs or the Department of Defense to Medicare-eligible beneficiaries in the calculation of an area's M+C capitation payment. This report will include, on a county-by-county basis: the actual or estimated costs of such services to Medicareeligible beneficiaries; the change in M+C capitation payment rates if such costs were included in the calculation of payment rates; one or more proposals for the implementation of payment adjustments to M+C plans in counties where the payment rate has been affected due to failure to account for the cost of such services; and a system to ensure that when a M+C enrollee receives covered services through a facility of these Departments, there is an appropriate payment recovery to the Medicare program.

Subtitle B – Other Medicare+Choice Reforms

Section 611. Payments of Additional Amounts for New Benefits Covered During a Contract Term

The provision requires payment adjustments to M+C plans if a legislative change results in significant increased costs, similar to the requirements for adjusting payments due to significant increased costs resulting from National Coverage Determination (NCDs). In addition, this provision requires that cost projections and payment adjustments be based on actuarial estimates provided by the Chief Actuary of the Health Care Financing Administration.

Section 612. Restriction on Implementation of Significant New Regulatory Requirements Mid-Year

The provision precludes the Secretary from implementing, other than at the beginning of a calendar year, regulations that impose new, significant regulatory requirements on M+C organizations.

Section 613. Timely Approval of Marketing Material that Follows Model Marketing Language

The provision requires the Secretary to make decisions, within 10 days, approving or modifying marketing material used by M+C organizations, provided that the organization uses model language specified by the Secretary. This provision applies to marketing material submitted on or after January 1, 2001.

Section 614. Avoiding Duplicative Regulation

This provision further stipulates when Medicare law preempts state law or regulation from applying to M+C plans, by specifying that the term *benefit requirements* includes cost-sharing requirements. Second, the provision stipulates that state laws and regulations affecting marketing materials, and summaries and schedules of benefits regarding an M+C plan, will also be preempted by Medicare law.

Section 615. Election of Uniform Local Coverage Policy for Medicare+Choice Plan Covering Multiple Localities

An M+C organization offering a plan in an area with more than one local coverage policy may elect to have the local coverage policy for the part of the area that is most beneficial to M+C enrollees (as identified by the Secretary) apply to all M+C enrollees enrolled in the plan.

Section 616. Eliminating Health Disparities in Medicare+Choice Program

This provision expands the M+C quality assurance programs for M+C plans to include a separate focus on racial and ethnic minorities. The

Secretary is also required to report to Congress how the quality assurance programs focus on racial and ethnic minorities, within 2 years after enactment and biennially thereafter.

Section 617. Medicare+Choice Program Compatibility with Employer or Union Group Health Plans

In order to make the M+C program compatible with employer or union group health plans, this provision allows the Secretary to waive or modify requirements that hinder the design of, offering of, or enrollment in certain M+C plans. Plans included in the category are M+C plans under contract between M+C organizations and employers, labor organizations, or trustees of a fund established by employers and/or labor organizations.

Section 618. Special Medigap Enrollment Anti-Discrimination Provision for Certain Beneficiaries

This provision extends the period for Medigap enrollment for certain M+C enrollees affected by termination of coverage. For individuals enrolled in an M+C plan during a 12-month trial period, their trial period will begin again if they reenrolled in another M+C plan because of an involuntary termination. During this new trial period, they will retain their rights to enroll in a Medigap policy; however, the total time for a trial period can not exceed 2 years from the time they first enrolled in an M+C plan.

Section 619. Restoring Effective Date of Elections and Changes of Elections of Medicare+Choice Plans

This provision allows individuals who enroll in an M+C plan after the 10th day of the month to receive coverage beginning on the first day of the next calendar month, effective June 1, 2001.

Section 620. Permitting ESRD Beneficiaries to Enroll in Another Medicare+Choice Plan if the Plan in which they are Enrolled is Terminated

This provision permits ESRD beneficiaries to enroll in another M+C plan if they lost coverage when their plan terminated its contract or reduced its service area. This provision is also retroactive, to include individuals whose enrollment in an M+C plan was terminated involuntarily on or after December 31, 1998.

Section 621. Providing Choice for Skilled Nursing Facility Services Under The Medicare+Choice Program

Effective for M+C contracts entered into or renewed on or after the date of enactment, the provision requires an M+C plan to cover post-hospitalization skilled nursing care through an enrollee's "home skilled nursing facility" if the plan has a contract with the facility or if the home facility agrees to accept substantially similar payment under the same terms and conditions that apply to similarly situated SNFs that are under contract with the plan. A "home skilled nursing facility" is defined as (a) one in which the enrollee resided at the time of the hospital admission that triggered eligibility for SNF care upon discharge, or (b) is the facility that is providing such services through the continuing care retirement community in which the enrollee resided at the time of hospital admission, or (c) is the facility in which the spouse of the enrollee is residing at the time of the enrollee's hospital discharge. SNF care at the home facility can be no less favorable than care received in another SNF that has a contract with the plan.

Home skilled nursing facilities are permitted to refuse to accept Medicare+Choice enrollees or to impose conditions on their acceptance of such an enrollee.

The provision requires the Medicare Payment Advisory Commission (MedPAC) to analyze and, within 2 years of enactment, report to Congress on the effects of this provision on the scope of benefits, administrative and other costs incurred by M+C organizations, and the contractual relationships between those plans and SNFs.

Section 622. Providing for Accountability of Medicare+Choice Plans

The provision mandates review of ACR submissions by the HCFA Chief Actuary with respect to submissions for ACRs filed on or after May 1, 2001.

Section 623. Increased Civil Money Penalty for Medicare+Choice Organizations that Terminate Contracts Mid-Year

This provision allows for a civil money penalty of up to $100,000 (or higher as established by the Secretary of Health and Human Services through regulations) for an M+C organization that terminates its contract other than at an appropriate time after providing appropriate notice.

Subtitle C – Other Managed Care Reforms

Section 631. 1-Year Extension of Social Health Maintenance Organization (SHMO) Demonstration Project

The provision extends SHMO waivers until 30 months after the Secretary submits a report with a plan for integration and transition of SHMOs into an option under the M+C program. This 30-month extension supersedes the 18-month extension in BBRA 99.

Section 632. Revised Terms and Conditions for Extension of Medicare Community Nursing Organization (CNO) Demonstration Project

Effective as if enacted with BBRA99, the provision eliminates the requirement that CNO capitated payments be reduced to ensure budget neutrality. Through December 2001, the projects will operate under the same terms and conditions applicable during 1999 but with modification to the capitation rates. From October 1, 2000, through December 31, 2000, the capitation rates will be adjusted for inflation since 1999 and for changes in service packages, but reduced by 10% for projects in Arizona, Minnesota, and Illinois and by 15% in New York. In 2001, the rates will be determined by actuarially adjusting the rates in the prior period for inflation, utilization, and changes to the service package. Adjustments will be made to case management fees for certain frail enrollees, and requirements will be imposed to create greater uniformity in clinical features among participating sites and to improve quality and enrollee satisfaction.

By July 1, 2001, the Secretary is required to submit to the House Committees on Ways and Means and Commerce and the Senate Committee on Finance a report evaluating the projects for the period July 1997 through December 1999 and for the extension period after September 30, 2000. A final report is required by July 1, 2002. The provision requires certain methods to be used to compare spending per beneficiary under the projects.

Section 633. Extension of Medicare Municipal Health Services Demonstration Projects

The provision extends the Medicare municipal health services demonstration projects for 2 additional years, through December 31, 2004.

Section 634. Service Area Expansion for Medicare Cost Contracts During Transition Period

This provision allows service area expansion for Medicare cost contracts, if the request was submitted to the Secretary before September 1, 2003.

Title IX – Other Provisions

Subtitle A – Pace Program

Section 901. Extension of Transition for Current Waivers

The provision permits the Secretary to continue to operate the Program of All-Inclusive Care for the Elderly (PACE) under waivers for a period of 36 months (rather than 24 months), and states may do so for 4 years (rather than 3 years). OBRA 86 required the Secretary to grant waivers of certain Medicare and Medicaid requirements to not more than 10 public or non-profit private community-based organizations to provide health and long-term care services on a capitated basis to frail elderly persons at risk of institutionalization. BBA 97 established PACE as a permanent provider under Medicare and as a special benefit under Medicaid.

Section 902. Continuing of Certain Operating Arrangements Permitted

If, prior to becoming a permanent component of Medicare, a PACE demonstration project had contractual or other operating arrangements that are not recognized under permanent program regulations, the provision requires the Secretary, in consultation with the state agency, to permit it to continue under such arrangements as long as it is consistent with the objectives of the PACE program.

Section 903. Flexibility in Exercising Waiver Authority

The provision enables the Secretary to exercise authority to modify or waive Medicare or Medicaid requirements to respond to the needs of PACE programs related to employment and the use of community care physicians. The Secretary must approve requests for such waivers within 90 days of the date the request for waiver is received.

Subtitle B – Outreach to Low-Income Medicare Beneficiaries

Section 911. Outreach on Availability of Medicare Cost-Sharing Assistance to Eligible Low-Income Medicare Beneficiaries

The provision requires the Commissioner of the Social Security Administration to conduct outreach efforts to identify individuals who may be eligible for Medicaid payment of Medicare cost sharing and to notify these persons of the availability of such assistance. The Commissioner must also furnish, at least annually, a list of such individuals who reside in each state to that state's agency responsible for administering the Medicaid program as well as to any other appropriate state agency. The list must include the name and address and whether such individuals have experienced reductions in Social Security benefits. The provision also requires the General Accounting Office to conduct a study of the impact of the outreach activities of the Commissioner to submit to Congress no later than 18 months after such outreach begins. The provision is effective one year after date of enactment.

Subtitle E – Information on Nursing Facility Staffing

Section 941. Posting of Information on Nursing Facility Staffing.

The provision requires Medicare skilled nursing facilities and Medicaid nursing facilities to post nurse staffing information daily for each shift in the facility, effective January 1, 2003.

Chapter 3

REACHING LOW-INCOME, UNINSURED CHILDREN: ARE MEDICAID AND SCHIP DOING THE JOB?[+]

Elicia Herz and Evelyne P. Baumrucker

INTRODUCTION

Congress has shown an on-going commitment to improving children's access to health care as demonstrated through eligibility expansions of the Medicaid program since the 1980s, and the introduction of the State Children's Health Insurance Program (SCHIP) in the fall of 1997. The majority of poor and near poor children are financially eligible for one of these programs.

Until recently, there was general disappointment with the implementation progress under SCHIP, due to low enrollment rates early in the program. Furthermore, after steady increases in the early 1990s, Medicaid caseloads showed an aggregate decline between 1995 and 1997. By FY2000, the pace of enrollment under SCHIP had improved, and data for 1998-1999 suggest that the decline in Medicaid participation may be reversing.

[+] Excerpted from CRS Report RL30556.

States have instituted a variety of outreach activities to bring eligible children into these two programs. Substantial progress has been made in simplifying the application and enrollment process under SCHIP, and also to a lesser extent under Medicaid. Budget limitations require state administrators to think carefully about their choice of outreach and enrollment facilitation strategies. However, current research assessing the cost-effectiveness of these strategies is inconclusive. Future state and federal evaluations of both Medicaid and SCHIP may start to identify what works, what does not, for whom, and at what cost.

Outreach funding is structured very differently under Medicaid and SCHIP. Medicaid does not have a specific limit on program spending for outreach, although the federal matching rate for such administrative activities can be lower than that for direct services. To date, there has been relatively low use by states of a special $500 million fund for Medicaid outreach to children losing welfare. For federal matching purposes under SCHIP, there is a limit on spending for administrative expenses including outreach and education. This cap in a given fiscal year is 10% of the amount states actually spend on benefits, rather than 10% of appropriated levels. Recent legislation changes SCHIP outreach funding.

Medicaid and SCHIP enrollment patterns are affected by complex interactions between economic trends, federal and state policies, program administrative procedures, and beneficiary perceptions. These interactions result in enormous enrollment variability across states, suggesting that some solutions may need to be state-specific. Given significant reductions in Medicaid enrollment among adults with children, some have argued that providing Medicaid and SCHIP to whole families may be a more effective mechanism for reducing the number of low-income children without health insurance than the current fractured set of eligibility rules. Further simplification of such rules, streamlining enrollment processes, and additional outreach are also important to improving coverage rates. These goals must be balanced with budget constraints that may result from any future economic downturns that may increase the number of individuals eligible for, and enrolling in these programs.

OVERVIEW

Research indicates that children are healthier when they get medical care. Health insurance improves access to these services. Congress has shown an on-going commitment to improving access to health care for poor and near-poor children. This commitment has been demonstrated through expansions of the Medicaid program since the 1980s and the establishment of the State Children's Health Insurance Program (SCHIP) in the fall of 1997.

Nonetheless, recent trends in insurance coverage among children are cause for concern. The number of children covered by health insurance rose to 86% in 1999. Still, 10.8 million children – 14% of all children under age 19 – were without health insurance in 1999, down from 11.9 million uninsured children in 1998.[1] In the 106th Congress, several bills were passed (and signed into law) to further expand eligibility for children under Medicaid, and to change existing provisions that govern outreach funding under SCHIP.

This report provides general background information on the current status of eligibility, enrollment, and outreach issues for children under Medicaid and SCHIP. We analyze recent enrollment statistics and factors contributing to those trends. Several issues concerning enrollment facilitation and outreach strategies are also discussed, including: (1) current approaches used by states under Medicaid and SCHIP, (2) research on effectiveness and cost-effectiveness of outreach and enrollment facilitation, (3) current funding for outreach under Medicaid and SCHIP, and related privately-financed efforts, and (4) legislative changes made during the 106th Congress to major outreach and eligibility provisions under Medicaid and SCHIP.

ELIGIBILITY AND ENROLLMENT OF CHILDREN UNDER MEDICAID AND SCHIP

Major Medicaid Eligibility Pathways for Children

Medicaid is a means-tested entitlement program. To qualify, applicants' income and resources[2] must be within program financial standards. These

---

[1] CRS Report 97-975 EPW, *Health Insurance Coverage of Children*, by Madeleine Smith.
[2] For most eligibility categories in most states, individuals must have resources (also called assets) valued at less than a specified amount (typically $1,000 for an adult with one or more dependent children) to be eligible for Medicaid. States determine what items constitute countable resources and how those countable items are valued. Resources such as homes and wedding rings are generally not counted, regardless of their value. Other types of resources,

standards vary considerably among states, and different standards apply to different population groups within a state. With some exceptions, Medicaid is available only to persons with very low incomes. In addition, Medicaid eligibility is subject to *categorical restrictions*. That is, it is available only to low-income persons who are aged, blind, disabled, members of families with dependent children, and certain other pregnant women and children.

The Medicaid statute defines over 50 distinct population groups as potentially eligible, including those for whom coverage is mandatory and those that states may elect to cover. Examples of *major mandatory coverage groups for children* include:

- Those meeting the financial and categorical criteria under the former Aid to Families with Dependent Children or AFDC program (as of July 16, 1996), even if they do not qualify for cash grants under the new Temporary Assistance for Needy Families (TANF) program.[3] Income standards here are typically well below the federal poverty level (FPL). For example, the maximum AFDC payment levels on July 16, 1996 ranged from 15% of the 1998 FPL in Alabama to 81% in Connecticut. The median level nationwide was 45%.[4]

- Children under age 6 years (and pregnant women) with family incomes below 133% FPL.

- In FY2001, children between the ages of 6 and 17 years living in families with income up to 100% FPL.

- Disabled children meeting the disability and income criteria for the Supplemental Security Income (SSI) program.[5]

---

such as cars, savings accounts and savings bonds, are generally counted. However, the entire value of these countable resources may not be considered. For example, up to $1,500 in equity value of the first car may be disregarded. (See Schneider, et al. *Medicaid Eligibility for Families and Children.* Washington, D.C., The Kaiser Commission on Medicaid and the Uninsured, September 1998.)

[3] Within certain federal restrictions, states may modify these financial standards for AFDCrelated groups (e.g., make such standards more or less restrictive than those in place on July 16, 1996).

[4] See Appendix Table 1 in Schneider, et al. *Medicaid Eligibility for Families and Children.* Washington, D.C., The Kaiser Commission on Medicaid and the Uninsured, September 1998.

[5] States may use more restrictive eligibility standards for Medicaid than those used for SSI if they were using those standards on January 1, 1972 (before implementation of SSI). These

Examples of major optional coverage groups for children include:

- Infants under age one year (and pregnant women) whose family income is no more than 185% FPL.

- The medically needy, persons who do not meet the financial standards for cash assistance programs but meet the categorical standards and have income and resources within specified medically needy limits established by the states. The income limits here can be as high as 133 and 1/3% of the corresponding AFDC payment standard (in effect on July 16, 1996, or as subsequently modified). Some children qualify for this coverage group when medical expenses are subtracted from family income and the net amount falls below the specified income standard.

Transitional or extended benefits are available to families who lose Medicaid eligibility due to increased earnings or child support payments.[6] States have the option of continuing Medicaid eligibility for current child beneficiaries for up to 12 months without a redetermination of eligibility. States are also allowed to extend Medicaid coverage to children under 19 years of age on the basis of "presumptive" eligibility until formal determinations are completed.

In addition to SCHIP (discussed below), other provisions in federal law allow states to extend Medicaid eligibility to children beyond federal requirements. For example, states have used less restrictive methodologies for determining countable income permitted under Section 1902(r)(2) of the Social Security Act to cover children in higher income families. States may also obtain special waivers of eligibility rules under Section 1115 of the same Act to cover new groups and/or change income criteria.

The first four columns of **Table 1** display Medicaid income eligibility criteria as a percentage of the FPL by age group and state. These criteria

---

states may vary in their definition of disability, or in their standards related to income or resources. Currently 11 states use these more restrictive standards.

[6] Specifically, when Medicaid eligibility via old AFDC rules is lost due to hours of or income from employment, or loss of a time-limited earned income disregard (and the family qualified for Medicaid on the basis of old AFDC rules in at least 3 of the preceding 6 months), states are required to continue Medicaid for the subsequent 6 months. States must extend Medicaid for an additional 6 months for families that were covered during the entire first 6-month period, and are earning below 185% FPL. Finally, certain families who lose

were in effect prior to implementation of SCHIP, which provides funding to states to cover children at income levels higher than those in place under their Medicaid programs. Overall, by early 1997, many states had expanded Medicaid eligibility for selected subgroups of children beyond the federal mandates. For example, 33 states had exceeded the federal minimum of 133% FPL for infants. Likewise, nine states extended eligibility for children ages 1 through 5 above this same mandatory minimum. Finally, 25 states moved beyond the federal mandate of 100% FPL and/or age requirements for children ages 6 and older.

Eligibility for SCHIP

Since the enactment of Medicaid in 1965, the State Children's Health Insurance Program represents the largest federal effort to provide health insurance coverage to uninsured, low-income children. SCHIP was established by the Balanced Budget Act of 1997 (BBA 97) under a new Title XXI of the Social Security Act. This block grant program provides funding to states to provide children with health insurance that meets specific standards for benefits and cost-sharing, or through their Medicaid programs, or through a combination of both.[7] Like Medicaid, SCHIP is a federalstate matching program. The federal medical assistance percentage (FMAP) that determines the federal contribution towards Medicaid spending ranges from 50% to 76.82% across states in FY2001. The enhanced FMAP for SCHIP ranges from 65% to 83.77%.

Title XXI defines SCHIP-eligible children as those who are not eligible for Medicaid or covered under a group health plan or other insurance. The law requires that states cover children in families with incomes that are either: (1) above the state's Medicaid financial eligibility standard but less than 200% of the FPL, or (2) in states with Medicaid income levels for children already at or above 200% FPL, within 50 percentage points over the state's current Medicaid income eligibility limit for children.

Not all targeted low-income children will necessarily receive medical assistance under SCHIP for two reasons. First, the law does not establish an

---

Medicaid because of increased child or spousal support are eligible for a 4-month extension of coverage if they received Medicaid in at least 3 of the preceding 6 months.

[7] Under limited circumstances, states have the option to purchase a health benefits plan that is provided by a community-based health delivery system, or to purchase family coverage under a group health plan as long as it is cost-effective to do so.

individual entitlement to the benefits of the SCHIP program.[8] Instead, it entitles *states* with approved SCHIP plans to a pre-determined, annual federal allotment based on a formula set in law. Second, each state can define the group of targeted low-income children who may enroll in SCHIP. Title XXI allows states to use the following factors in determining eligibility: geography, age, income and resources, residency, disability status (so long as any standard relating to such status does not restrict eligibility), access to other health insurance, and duration of eligibility for SCHIP coverage.

As of December 11, 2000, the Health Care Financing Administration (HCFA) had approved SCHIP plans for all 50 states, the District of Columbia and five territories. Twenty-one states expanded their Medicaid programs for children, 16 used separate state programs to provide children with health insurance, and 19 combined a Medicaid expansion and a separate state program. The upper income limit for Medicaid expansions and separate state programs under SCHIP has reached 350%[9] of the poverty level in one state (**Table 1**).

While expansions in coverage have been achieved for children of all ages under SCHIP, the most significant increases in eligibility have benefitted older adolescents. Under Medicaid in FY2001, states must cover children ages 6 to 17 in families with incomes up to 100% FPL. The age of mandatory coverage increases to 18 in 2002. Under SCHIP, most states have taken advantage of the opportunity to cover older teens in families with incomes up to 100% FPL (or often higher) *sooner* than required under Medicaid. Such states will receive an enhanced federal matching rate through SCHIP to finance the care provided to these older adolescents (until mandatory coverage under regular Medicaid applies).

---

[8] The one exception to this rule is when a state chooses to implement a Medicaid expansion under SCHIP. Children enrolled in SCHIP through a Medicaid expansion are entitled to Medicaid benefits as long as they continue to meet these specific eligibility criteria (even if SCHIP itself terminates) or until the state is granted approval to eliminate the eligibility category created by the Medicaid expansion under SCHIP.

[9] For determining income eligibility for SCHIP and Medicaid, some states apply "income disregards." These are specified dollar amounts subtracted from gross income to compute net income, that is then compared to the applicable income criterion. Such disregards *increase* the *effective* income level above the stated standard. State SCHIP plans do not consistently report use of income disregards, nor whether the stated income standards include or exclude such disregards.

Recent Trends in Program Enrollment among Children under Medicaid and SCHIP

There is some recent evidence and considerable speculation that both Medicaid and SCHIP may be underutilized by currently eligible children. Analyses of 1994-1997 national survey data indicate that 21 to 42% of all uninsured children under 18 years of age are eligible for Medicaid but not enrolled.[10] The U.S. General Accounting Office (GAO)[11] found that, in 1997, compared to Medicaid-enrolled children of similar ages, uninsured children eligible for, but not enrolled in, Medicaid were more likely to be in working families, Hispanic and either U.S.-born to foreign-born parents or foreign-born themselves. They were also more likely to live in the West and the South – 73% of all uninsured Medicaid-eligible children nationwide resided in these regions. In a more recent analysis,[12] in 1999, there were 7.1 million uninsured children under 19 years of age living in families with incomes below 200% of the federal poverty level. Of this group, 6.7 million, or 94% would have met their state's eligibility criteria under Medicaid or SCHIP based on the rules in place as of July 2000.

While current eligibility rules under these two publicly financed programs permit coverage for most low-income children, during the 1990s, actual enrollment fluctuated for a number of reasons. Between 1990 and 1995, Medicaid participation increased an average of 7.6% per year.[13] These increases were the result of a combination of factors. During this period, the economy was weak, increasing the number of low-income individuals and families who qualified for Medicaid. In addition, during the latter half of the 1980s, Congress established the new poverty-related eligibility categories for pregnant women and children which continued to produce significant

---

[10] See Table 7 in Lewis, K., M. Ellwood, and J. Czajka. *Counting the Uninsured: A Review of the Literature.* Washington, D.C., The Urban Institute, June 1998. The wide variation in the estimate of uninsured children eligible for Medicaid is due to methodological differences across reviewed studies in definitions of the target population, data sources and statistical analysis models.

[11] U.S. General Accounting Office. Medicaid: Demographics of Nonenrolled Children Suggest State Outreach Strategies. GAO/HEHS-98-93, March 1998. Washington, 1998. (Hereafter cited as GAO, Medicaid: Demographics of Nonenrolled Children)

[12] Broaddus, M., and Ku, L. *Nearly 95 Percent of Low-Income Uninsured Children Now are Eligible for Medicaid or SCHIP.* Washington, D.C., Center on Budget and Policy Priorities, December 6, 2000.

[13] Information presented here on trends in Medicaid enrollment and welfare participation during the early 1990s is taken from Ku, L., and Bruen, B. *The Continuing Decline in Medicaid Coverage* (Series A, No. A-37), Washington, D.C., The Urban Institute, December 1999.

enrollment increases during the early 1990s. Similarly, coverage of new groups of disabled children resulted from expansions of eligibility for the Supplemental Security Income (SSI) program[14] which in turn confers automatic Medicaid eligibility in most states.

Trends in Medicaid enrollment changed by the mid-1990s **(Table 2)**. A total of 41.3 million people in the 50 states and the District of Columbia were enrolled in Medicaid during 1996, a small decrease from the total of 41.7 million people enrolled in 1995. By 1997, enrollment had declined to 40.6 million. The rate of continuing decline in Medicaid participation had slowed by 1998, during which there were 40.4 million enrollees.

Enrollment patterns for this period varied by eligibility group. Between 1995 and 1998, the total number of able-bodied adults (typically parents) and children on Medicaid fell (with one exception described below), while the number of aged beneficiaries stayed roughly constant, and the number of disabled of all ages rose slightly. As shown on **Table 2**, for adults and children, reductions were greatest among those eligible for Medicaid via welfare or cash-related pathways. However, these losses were partially offset by increases in enrollment through other eligibility pathways.[15]

Over this 4-year period, adults qualifying for Medicaid via cash-related groups fell 36%, while enrollment in other groups rose by nearly 24%, yielding a net loss for adults of 10%. There was a small increase in the number of adults between 1997 and 1998. New York had added 300,000 adults to its Medicaid program via an expansion of its §1115 waiver to include the state's pre-existing Home Relief (health insurance) program. In addition, Massachusetts added thousands of adults to Medicaid through an 1115 waiver implemented in 1998. When these two state-specific expansions are discounted, nationwide enrollment of adults actually dropped by approximately 400,000 in 1998.[16]

Declines in enrollment were also observed for children, but the losses were less severe. Between 1995 and 1998, children qualifying for Medicaid under cash-related groups dropped by 32%, while other Medicaid enrollment

---

[14] For example, the Supreme Court's 1990 decision in Sullivan v. Zebley broadened SSI eligibility for children, particularly those with learning disabilities.

[15] Other enrollment is likely to be a combination of new beneficiaries and individuals who no longer qualify for Medicaid via old AFDC rules (after welfare reform), but who continue (or reinstate) their Medicaid coverage through alternative pathways such as poverty-related eligibility categories, medically needy groups, transitional Medicaid, or through §1115 waiver programs.

[16] Unpublished Urban Institute analysis (results will be forthcoming in a report to be published by the Kaiser Commission on Medicaid and the Uninsured).

increased by 25%, resulting in a smaller net reduction for children of nearly 5%. These patterns of enrollment loss for adults and children reflect the fact that more Medicaid eligibility pathways exist for children, and these pathways use more generous income criteria, compared to eligibility options for nondisabled adults.

The declines in Medicaid caseloads for adults and children between 1995 and 1998 are likely the result of several concomitant events. During this period, an improved economy and higher employment rates increased the number of individuals not meeting income-related criteria for Medicaid eligibility. However, there has been considerable speculation that the primary cause of the drop in Medicaid participation has been federal welfare reform under the Personal Responsibility and Work Opportunity Reconciliation Act of 1996 (PRWORA). But in fact, prior to enactment of PRWORA, both Medicaid and welfare caseloads had already begun to fall, and most states had already implemented major welfare reform initiatives under waivers of federal law. Moreover, PRWORA included provisions to prevent the automatic loss of Medicaid coverage due to the loss of cash assistance. However, as the data reported above suggest, these provisions may not have been completely effective. TANF exit studies do not directly assess reasons for the drop in Medicaid enrollment, but some of the possible contributing factors identified in these studies include, for example, failure to identify eligible families, lack of awareness of the availability of continuing Medicaid coverage, and agency errors. In addition, some caseload declines may have resulted from family members no longer being eligible for Medicaid.[17]

Other research[18] documents related reasons why families do not enroll their children in Medicaid, including:

- families lack knowledge of Medicaid and its eligibility criteria;

- families may not perceive a need for Medicaid due to good health and alternative sources of care;

---

[17] See Greenberg, M. *Participation in Welfare and Medicaid Enrollment.* Washington, D.C., Kaiser Commission on Medicaid and the Uninsured, September 1998. Another study on this issue is Health Management Associates. *The Dynamics of Current Medicaid Enrollment Changes.* Washington, D.C., Kaiser Commission on Medicaid and the Uninsured, October 1998.

[18] GAO, Medicaid: Demographics of Nonenrolled Children; and the Kaiser Commission on Medicaid and the Uninsured. *Medicaid and Children; Overcoming Barriers to Enrollment, Findings from a National Survey.* Washington, D.C., January 2000.

- some have concerns about quality of care and low levels of provider participation limiting access;

- cultural differences, language barriers and immigration policies may prevent some families from enrolling in Medicaid;

- for many, Medicaid has a negative image associated with its historical ties to cash assistance and thus the stigma of dependency; and,

- the enrollment process itself, with long forms and extensive documentation, can be a barrier.

A recent analysis published by the Kaiser Commission[19] examining monthly Medicaid enrollment patterns in the 50 states and the District of Columbia suggests that the decline in Medicaid participation may be reversing itself. Comparing December of 1998 to December of 1999, Medicaid enrollment grew by 1.1 million, or 3.6%, with 43 states and the District of Columbia experiencing growth. As with the 1995-1998 trends reported previously, this analysis revealed enormous variability in enrollment across states.

Even though overall enrollment rose, patterns of enrollment within eligibility groups in this study mirrored national results reported for the 1995-1998 period. Enrollment among the aged and disabled (data from 43 states) steadily increased by 1.6% for the year ending December 1998, and 1.8% for the year ending December 1999. For families, children and pregnant women, continuing large decreases in cashrelated enrollment were offset by increases in enrollment through other eligibility pathways. For example, among the 21 states with data for families, children and pregnant women, cash-related enrollment declined by 18.9% over the year ending December 1998 and by 16.6% over the year ending December 1999. In contrast, among 22 states with data, poverty-related groups experienced an

---

[19] Ellis, E., Smith, V., and Rousseau, D. *Medicaid Enrollment in 50 States.* Washington, D.C.: The Kaiser Commission on Medicaid and the Uninsured. October 2000. This study is based on monthly enrollment reports for the months of June and December of 1997, 1998 and 1999. These point-in-time estimates do not match official HCFA data which describe the number of persons ever enrolled in a given fiscal year. Estimates from this study are smaller than HCFA's official counts of enrollees. In addition to examining overall trends in enrollment by state, this study also analyzed enrollment changes by eligibility group, however, data were not available from some states for each category.

increase of 9.4% in 1998 and 14.0% in 1999. On April 7, 2000, HCFA instructed states to institute necessary policy and procedural changes to identify, enroll, and re-enroll families and children who may have been improperly denied coverage under, or terminated from Medicaid. Of most concern are beneficiaries who are denied Medicaid due to ineligibility for TANF, lose Medicaid when TANF ends, or lose transitional Medicaid without proper notice or redetermination. States were directed to focus also on children inappropriately dropped from Medicaid after they lost SSI payments due to changes in SSI disability rules under welfare reform. States are required to develop a timetable for redeterminations and conducting additional eligibility reviews as necessary for these target populations.

Concerns about underutilization have also been raised about SCHIP. SCHIP faces all the start-up issues confronting a relatively new program that is just over 3 years old. Early enrollment estimates from HCFA[20] indicated that nearly 1 million children (982,000) were enrolled in SCHIP under 43 operational state programs as of December 1998. More recently, HCFA reported that nearly 2 million children (1,979,450) were enrolled in SCHIP during FY1999 under 53 operational state programs.[21] Over 1.2 million of these children were served by separate programs and almost 700,000 were enrolled in Medicaid expansions. On January 5, 2001, the Clinton Administration announced that enrollment in the SCHIP program reached approximately 3.3 million children during FY2000, with 2.3 million children enrolled in separate state programs, and a little more than 1 million children enrolled in Medicaid expansion programs.[22] Subsequent to the enactment of BBA 97, CBO estimated that SCHIP would cover an average of 2.3 million children per year after 1999.[23] The Clinton Administration's goal was to enroll 5 million children in SCHIP by FY2002.

Spending projections in the first 2 years of the program are consistent with HCFA's enrollment figures and fall well below total federal appropriation levels. Federal spending in FY1998 totaled less than $500 million. Federal spending in FY1999 totaled approximately $1 billion.

---

[20] Health Care Financing Administration. A Preliminary Estimate of the Children's Health Insurance Program Aggregate Enrollment Numbers Through December 31, 1998 (background only). April 20, 1999.

[21] Health Care Financing Administration. The State Children's Health Insurance Program, Annual Enrollment Report, October 1, 1998-September 30, 1999 (no date).

[22] Bureau of National Affairs. HCFA Releases Final SCHIP Rule, As Clinton Notes 70% Participation Increase. *Health Care Daily Report*, v. 6, no. 5, January 8, 2001.

[23] U.S. Congressional Budget Office. Expanding Health Insurance Coverage for Children Under Title XXI of the Social Security Act (CBO Memorandum). February 1998.

Program spending is expected to accelerate over time. CBO estimates that federal SCHIP spending will total approximately $2 billion for FY2000 and $3 billion for FY2001[24] (although these estimates may be revised in CBO's new FY2001 baseline as a result of new enrollment data). For each of these years, total annual federal appropriation levels are approximately $4.3 billion.[25]

Federal law requires that eligibility for Medicaid and SCHIP be coordinated when states implement separate SCHIP programs. In these circumstances, applications for SCHIP coverage must first be screened for Medicaid eligibility. CBO estimates that the "outreach effect" of SCHIP will increase Medicaid enrollment by 460,000 children each year for FY1998 through FY2002. As a result, Medicaid spending is also expected to increase a total of $2.4 billion over this same 5-year period.[26] The Kaiser study described previously suggests that SCHIP is in fact facilitating Medicaid enrollment. Comparing monthly enrollment counts for December 1998 to December 1999, total Medicaid participation increased by 1.1 million. Twenty-seven percent of this increase was due to enrollment via expansions of Medicaid through SCHIP.

ENROLLMENT FACILITATION AND OUTREACH STRATEGIES

Successful enrollment penetration among all potential Medicaid and SCHIP eligible children will depend at least in part on two different, but interrelated activities – enrollment facilitation and outreach. How is enrollment facilitation different conceptually from outreach? The former includes strategies to simplify and expedite the eligibility determination and enrollment process (e.g., allowing applications to be submitted by mail or fax, eliminating resource or asset tests). The latter includes strategies to market the program to the target population so they will perceive the benefits

---

[24] U.S. Congressional Budget Office. *The Budget and Economic Outlook: An Update.* July 18, 2000. Washington, GPO, 2000.

[25] In general, annual allotments for each state will remain available for a period of 3 years. The period of availability for the FY1998 allotments ended as of October 1, 2000. Unspent funds for both FY1998 and FY1999 will be redistributed according to provisions contained in newly enacted legislation (P.L. 106-554). For a complete discussion of redistribution issues, see CRS Report RS20628, *State Children's Health Insurance Program (SCHIP): Funding Changes in the 106th Congress,* by Evelyne Baumrucker.

[26] GAO, Medicaid: Demographics of Nonenrolled Children.

of participation and initiate the application process (e.g., advertising through radio, television and print media, establishing toll-free hotlines).[27] Some activities can be classified as both (e.g., placing eligibility workers in non-welfare settings frequented by the target population, involving local businesses and community-based organizations in outreach and enrollment efforts).

Ideally, mechanisms to simplify and expedite enrollment for families with eligible children are put into place prior to launching targeted outreach strategies.[28] In practice, however, both types of activities may evolve and occur in tandem over time as barriers to enrollment and outreach are identified, and solutions are designed and implemented.

Outreach and Enrollment Facilitation Strategies Used by States Under Medicaid and SCHIP

In an analysis of SCHIP state plans and amendments as of September 30, 1999 for the 50 states, the District of Columbia, and five territories,[29] eight common outreach strategies to market SCHIP to targeted populations were identified. Nearly all jurisdictions:

- involve health care providers in their educational efforts (54 jurisdictions);

- conduct radio, TV and print media campaigns to educate the target population (53 jurisdictions);

- develop partnerships with schools to reach eligible children (52 jurisdictions);

- use toll-free hotlines (52 jurisdictions); and,

- place eligibility workers in strategic locations such as sporting events, tax assistance sites, or free health clinics (50 jurisdictions).

---

[27] National Governors' Association. Center for Best Practices, and the National Conference of State Legislatures. *State Children's Health Insurance Program, 1999 Annual Report*, 1999. (Hereafter cited as National Governors' Association, *State Children's Health Insurance Program*.)

[28] Alliance for Health Reform. Health Coverage: Outreach to Uninsured Kids. May 1998.

[29] National Governors' Association, State Children's Health Insurance Program.

One-half to two-thirds of jurisdictions also:

- use a family-friendly website (39 jurisdictions);
- work with local employers to promote SCHIP (34 jurisdictions); and,
- involve the business community in their outreach efforts (32 jurisdictions).

Accurate identification of the target population upon which to focus outreach efforts is extremely difficult. Participation in other government programs may provide a vehicle for such identification. Using data from the 1997 National Survey of America's Families, the Urban Institute[30] estimates that 73% of all uninsured children who live in families with incomes below 200% FPL participate in the National School Lunch program, the Special Supplemental Nutrition Program for Women, Infants and Children (WIC), the Food Stamp program, or the Unemployment Compensation program. Among these programs, the National School Lunch program has the greatest penetration rate, serving roughly 60% of such children. In late 1999, President Clinton asked the Secretaries of HHS and Agriculture to identify effective school-based outreach strategies for possible replication throughout the country.[31]

With respect to enrollment facilitation, federal law stipulates few documentation requirements for determining eligibility under Medicaid, and even fewer requirements under SCHIP.[32] And the burden of required verification lies with state agencies rather than with families, although states may choose to shift some of this responsibility to families. States must obtain the Social Security number of children applying for Medicaid – such information is *not* required under SCHIP. Income and assets may be established through self-declaration under both programs. However, under

---

[30] Kenney, G., J. Haley, and F. Ullman. *Most Uninsured Children are in Families Served by Government Programs* (Policy Brief, Series B, No. B-4), Washington, D.C., The Urban Institute, December 1999.

[31] U.S. Dept. of Health and Human Services. *Report to the President: Interagency Task Force on Children's Health Insurance Outreach,* October 12, 1999. [http://www.hrsa.gov/childhealth/report.htm] Also see HCFA letter to SCHIP State Health Officials regarding school-based outreach, September 8, 2000.

[32] HCFA letter to SCHIP State Health Officials regarding application and enrollment simplification, September 10, 1998.

Medicaid only, subsequent to initial application, states must request information from other federal and state agencies to verify applicants' income and resources – such verification is *not* required under SCHIP. For both programs, children who are citizens may establish their citizenship through self-declaration; states are permitted to require further verification as a condition of eligibility. Children applying for either program who are qualified aliens must present documentation of their immigration status, which states must then verify with the Immigration and Naturalization Service. In sum, under Medicaid and even more so under SCHIP, states have enormous flexibility in facilitating application for and enrollment in these programs.

According to a recent national survey,[33] many states have implemented (or plan to implement) one or more enrollment facilitation strategies for children under Medicaid and SCHIP. In general, while substantial progress had been made to simplify and expedite enrollment, specific policies and procedures are more likely to have been adopted in separate SCHIP programs than in Medicaid programs **(Table 3)**. Detailed findings from this study include the following:

- At the initial application stage, the majority of states with separate SCHIP programs have implemented joint Medicaid/SCHIP enrollment forms (87%). States are less likely to use joint applications at redeterminations (44%).

- The majority of all states have dropped asset tests (Medicaid-82%, separate SCHIP-97%) and eliminated face-to-face interviews (Medicaid-78%, separate SCHIP-97%). In most cases, as with initial applications, states forego face-toface interviews when redetermining eligibility (Medicaid-84%, separate SCHIP-100%).

- Subsequent to initial application, about one-fourth of Medicaid programs (27%) and over two-thirds of separate SCHIP programs (69%) provide 12 months of continuous coverage without regard to changes in family income. These same states provide 12 months of continuous enrollment at redetermination of eligibility.

---

[33] Ross, D., and Cox, L. Making It Simple: Medicaid for Children and CHIP Income Eligibility Guidelines and Enrollment Procedures: Findings from a 50-State Survey. Washington, D.C., The Kaiser Commission on Medicaid and the Uninsured, October 2000.

- A small number of states allow presumptive eligibility[34] under Medicaid (16%) and SCHIP (13%).

- Few programs allow self-declaration of income (Medicaid-20%, separate SCHIP-22%) during the eligibility determination process.

Finally, in some states, the application, enrollment and redetermination procedures may depend on the point of entry into Medicaid or SCHIP. The findings described above typically characterize state processes associated with joint applications used to determine initial eligibility for Medicaid or separate SCHIP programs. Families initially applying for health coverage through Medicaid or welfare offices, particularly those families seeking coverage for adults as well as children, are likely to encounter a different, often more complicated application, enrollment and redetermination process.

Research on Effectiveness and Cost-Effectiveness of Selected Outreach and Enrollment Facilitation Strategies

Since the initiation of SCHIP a little over 3 years ago, states have struggled to develop and implement the "right" combination of outreach strategies and enrollment facilitation processes to maximize program participation. The advent of SCHIP has also focused attention on a variety of Medicaid enrollment issues.

Anecdotal evidence about the best combination of strategies to increase enrollment abounds in newspaper articles, speeches and the research literature. Given the unscientific nature of this type of evidence, it is perhaps not surprising that resulting conclusions about which states are or will be successful are often inconsistent. And such conclusions change over time as state strategies evolve. Since anecdotal evidence has many limitations, what types of data are better? How do we determine the effectiveness of different outreach and enrollment strategies? And finally, what are the costs

---

[34] Presumptive eligibility allows children whose family income appears to be below the state's Medicaid income guidelines to enroll temporarily in Medicaid, until a final formal determination of eligibility is made. At the time of the survey summarized in the text, there was no explicit presumptive eligibility provision in SCHIP law. Nonetheless, through other Title XXI authority, HCFA allowed states to implement similar procedures under this program. A recent law makes Medicaid presumptive eligibility provisions applicable to separate (non-Medicaid) SCHIP programs.

associated with effective outreach and enrollment activities – what strategies provide the biggest bang for the buck?

To answer these questions, in the summer of 1999, we searched the research literature for studies examining the effectiveness or cost-effectiveness of various outreach and enrollment facilitation strategies used to bring families or children into basic health care programs. While a large number of studies were identified initially for possible inclusion in our analysis, we found few well-designed studies from which reliable and valid conclusions could be drawn. And those analyses were only indirectly related to our purpose – rather than assessing changes in rates of program enrollment among non-participants as a result of outreach, these studies examined changes in use of specific preventive services (e.g., well-child visits and immunizations) subsequent to outreach targeting children already enrolled in a health care program or physician practice group. Results from studies examining the effectiveness of outreach in increasing use of key preventive services among program participants may not be generalizable to outreach aimed at increasing program enrollment.[35] Service utilization may be a less complicated process than the process of applying for coverage under Medicaid or SCHIP. In addition, the perceived (and actual) benefits of service use may be more immediate and obvious than benefits associated with qualifying for health insurance.

Finally, it was difficult to compare findings and draw conclusions from the few well-designed studies that we did find because they: (1) assessed different outreach strategies (e.g., home visits, telephone contacts, letters), (2) used different comparison groups (e.g., interventions were sometimes compared to no intervention or alternative strategies), (3) focused on different populations of children, and typically did not stratify results by subgroup (e.g., infants versus school-age children) to pinpoint variations in outreach effectiveness, and (4) measured different outcomes to evaluate the impact of a given outreach strategy (e.g., percent of eligibles reached/contacted versus percent of eligibles enrolled). Reported costs per "successful" case reached, enrolled or served varied dramatically across the few studies that attempted to quantify such cost-effectiveness. The variations in reported costs per successful case were due both to the modest effectiveness of outreach strategies investigated and the wide variability in

---

[35] Barents Group LLC. *Review of the Literature on Evaluations of Outreach for Public Health Insurance and Selected Other Programs (Final Report)*, prepared for the Agency for Healthcare Quality and Research (Contract No. 290-96-0004). Washington, D.C., Barents Group LLC, February 18, 2000.

the components included in calculating outreach costs (e.g., labor, computer hardware and software purchases, travel, training, office space rental, supplies).

Our conclusions about the status of research in this area were confirmed by a comprehensive review of the literature sponsored by the Agency for Healthcare Research and Quality (AHRQ).[36] This review concluded that very few outreach interventions have been evaluated, and that completed evaluations provide minimal scientific evidence about the absolute effectiveness, relative effectiveness[37] or costeffectiveness of different outreach and enrollment facilitation strategies for programs such as Medicaid and SCHIP. However, the analysis did identify three well-designed studies suggesting that simplified application procedures, aggressive outreach and/or presumptive eligibility for pregnant women positively impacted timely enrollment into Medicaid.

While it may be desirable to isolate and quantify the effectiveness of a given component of outreach or enrollment facilitation strategy, in the real world, states are implementing multiple activities simultaneously, making such assessments extremely difficult. It may be more practical and useful to assess the effectiveness of common combinations of strategies that may have broad application.

Current law requires an evaluation of each state's SCHIP program, designed to assess effectiveness in achieving the goals of the program. This evaluation was due in early 2000. To assist states in meeting this requirement, the National Academy for State Health Policy, a non-profit forum for state policy leaders, developed a model framework for the 2000 evaluation report. Because this model framework was designed to meet all statutory reporting requirements, HCFA encouraged states to use it, and all states and territories did so.

We conducted an informal review of these evaluation reports,[38] examining objectives related to reducing the number of uninsured children and improving SCHIP and Medicaid enrollment, as well as methods and indicators used to assess outreach effectiveness. In general, the reported data

---

[36] Ibid.
[37] Studies of absolute effectiveness compare an intervention to a control (no intervention). Studies of relative effectiveness compare two or more interventions to each other.
[38] Annual state SCHIP reports for FFY1998 are available for most states. Because SCHIP had just gotten started during this fiscal year, information on the effectiveness of outreach and enrollment processes in these reports are at best preliminary. States were allowed to combine their FY1999 annual reports and the 2000 evaluation reports as one comprehensive document.

are not typically tied to specific outreach or enrollment facilitation efforts. That is, the analyses reported describe overall success/failure of all activities (and other factors) combined. A wide variety of measures are reported, for example, percent of the targeted population enrolled, volume of hot line calls received subsequent to a media campaign, number of applications distributed and returned by source, specified geographic areas, and/or income groups.

Despite the use of a uniform reporting template, definitions of numerators and denominators for these measures, and time frames for analysis, varied widely, making direct comparisons among states extremely difficult. In assessing the percent of the target population enrolled, establishing a denominator–the estimate of eligible uninsured children–is clearly a major problem for many states. There are few reliable data sources, especially for small states for which major national surveys such as the Current Population Survey (CPS)[39] or the Survey of Income and Program Participation (SIPP) are inadequate. In response, some states have or are planning to conduct state-specific surveys to derive alternative estimates.

Additional evaluation data will be available in the near future. P. L. 106-113 authorizes a new 10-state federal evaluation that will include an assessment of effective and ineffective outreach and enrollment practices for both Medicaid and SCHIP; an analysis of Medicaid eligibility rules and procedures that are a barrier to enrollment in Medicaid, and how coordination between Medicaid and SCHIP has affected enrollment under both programs; and an analysis of disenrollment patterns and factors influencing this process. The Secretary must submit the results of this evaluation to Congress no later than December 31, 2001.

Current Funding for Outreach Under Medicaid and SCHIP

From a policy standpoint, outreach funding issues differ between Medicaid and SCHIP. For Medicaid, the main question is whether and how states are using administrative funds to reach and enroll eligible children. For SCHIP, the main issue is whether current limitations on outreach funding are a barrier to identification and enrollment of eligible children.

Medicaid does not have a specific limit on the proportion of program spending devoted to administrative activities such as outreach, although the

---

[39] CPS improvements are planned to remedy this situation. P.L. 106-113 included funding to support the collection of reliable annual state-by-state estimates on the number of children without health insurance, beginning in FY2000, and for each year thereafter.

federal matching rate for such administrative expenses can be lower than that for direct services.[40] In addition, there is a special $500 million fund established under the 1996 welfare reform legislation that provides higher federal matching rates for certain types of administrative expenses associated with Medicaid outreach to children losing welfare. This fund became available in FY1997.[41]

Despite the availability of these funds with federal matching rates of either 75% or 90% (depending on the outreach activity and allotment spending),[42] 45 states received only $195.6 million or 40% of the $500 million fund as of June, 2000.[43] According to a 1999 survey of 40 states,[44] many have used (or plan to use) this fund to support activities that qualify for a 90% match from the federal government, including for example, developing and disseminating new publications (19 states), training (18 states), outreach (16 states), outstationing of Medicaid eligibility workers (14 states), community activities (e.g., meetings and speeches; 14 states), public service announcements (13 states) and educational activities (12 states). Twenty-six of 40 states were also expecting to receive a 75% match for making necessary changes to their eligibility systems.

---

[40] Administrative expenses are generally matched at the rate of 50%. In FY2000, 41 of 56 states and territories had federal matching rates for services higher than 50%. In FY2001, 42 of 56 states and territories had federal matching rates for services higher than 50%.

[41] P.L. 106-113 lifted the FY2000 sunset on this fund and removed the requirement that states use this fund for administrative costs incurred only during the first 12 quarters subsequent to the effective date of their welfare reform programs.

[42] The $500 million fund is divided into two allocations for every state: a base allocation which is the same for all states ($2 million) and a secondary allocation that is distributed across the states based on four weighted factors. These factors include: (a) state AFDC-related caseload (60%), (b) state Medicaid administrative expenses (20%), (c) SSI childhood disability case reevaluations (10%), and (d) SSI immigrant caseload (10%). States may receive reimbursement at a 90% federal matching rate for expenditures claimed against their base allocation, and either 75% or 90% federal matching rate for expenditures claimed against their secondary allocation, depending on the type of activity. Examples of activities matched at 90% include public service announcements, placement of eligibility workers in new locations, and development and dissemination of new publications for at-risk populations. Activities that may be matched at either 90% or 75% (depending on whether claims are made against the base or secondary allocation, respectively) include, for example, hiring new eligibility workers for eligibility determinations related to welfare reform only, designing new eligibility forms, and eligibility system changes.

[43] Families USA. *TANF $500 Million De-Linking Fund*. [http://www.familiesusa.org/tanf_500.htm]

[44] Darnell, J., H. Lee, and J. Murdock. *Medicaid and Welfare Reform: States' Use of the $500 Million Federal Fund*. Washington, D.C., The Kaiser Commission on Medicaid and the Uninsured, October 1999.

Why has the $500 million fund been underutilized to date? Findings from the aforementioned 1999 survey of 40 states identify several issues. These states indicated that initial confusion about the appropriate uses (and previously applicable dates of expiration) of the $500 million fund created barriers to utilization. The regulations[45] delineating both the types of outreach expenses that qualify for enhanced matching and the required documentation for reimbursement are very complicated and thus, may also be burdensome. HCFA has issued a series of letters to State Medicaid Directors (most recently in early January 2000) to clarify permissible uses of this fund and proper claiming procedures. States also reported that competing priorities (e.g., implementation of SCHIP, Y2K, Medicaid managed care) and other external factors (e.g., need for legislative approval to implement new strategies) were obstacles to designing and implementing Medicaid outreach and enrollment activities.

Outreach funding under SCHIP is structured very differently from Medicaid and thus raises a different set of issues. For federal matching purposes under SCHIP, there is a limit on spending for administrative expenses including outreach and education. This limit or cap in a given fiscal year is equal to 10% of the amount states actually draw down from their allotments to cover benefits under SCHIP, as opposed to 10% of the appropriated level.

The current law allows flexibility in seeking federal payments for expenditures associated with outreach for SCHIP. For states that expand Medicaid under SCHIP, federal financial participation for related administration and outreach expenditures may be claimed either through Medicaid or SCHIP. To maximize federal payment, all states have the option to delay claiming administrative expenses under SCHIP up to 2 years from the date of the expenditure for the service. This option is designed to allow states with low benefit expenditures in the early years of the program to receive payments for associated administrative expenses over time at the enhanced federal matching rate.

The administrative costs of the Medicare and Medicaid programs rarely exceed 5% of total program costs. Based on that percentage, it would seem logical that a ceiling of 10% of program costs would be sufficient to administer an established program. Nonetheless, states have expressed concern over the SCHIP administrative funding cap and their ability to do

---

[45] Medicaid Program; Allocation of Enhanced Federal Matching Funds for Increased Administrative Costs Resulting From Welfare Reform. *Federal Register*, v. 62, no. 93, May

comprehensive outreach to achieve enrollment goals, especially early in the program.

Administrative costs tend to be higher during the initial start-up of a new program, compared with the costs of running an existing program. During the first 2 years after SCHIP was enacted, many states in the start-up phase of their programs found the 10% cap to be particularly burdensome. In an August 6, 1998 letter to State Health Officials, HCFA acknowledged that the 10% cap presented a problem for states. Indeed, of the 15 states that reported any administrative spending in FY1998, 6 reached the ceiling and claimed the full 10% of total spending for administrative costs.[46] By 1999, the portion of national SCHIP spending claimed for administrative costs had declined as a percentage of total program spending. To address state concerns about the cap on administrative spending under SCHIP, the 106th Congress passed legislation (incorporated into P.L. 106-554) that stipulates a redistribution formula for unspent FY1998 and FY1999 funds. This new provision further permits states that did not spend their full FY1998 allotments (within required time limits) to use up to 10% of retained FY1998 funds under the new redistribution formula specifically for outreach activities. These outreach funds are above and beyond funding available under the 10% cap for all SCHIP administrative expenses. States have until the end of FY2002 to use the retained funds.

Privately Funded Outreach Initiatives and Coordination With Medicaid and SCHIP

To supplement public funding, private funding has become available to help states implement new outreach initiatives targeted at children and adolescents. For example, the Robert Wood Johnson Foundation (RWJF) has established a new grant program called Covering Kids. This program will make a total of $47 million available to states over 3 years, starting in 1999. The funds are intended to help design and conduct outreach activities that identify and enroll eligible children into Medicaid and other programs such as SCHIP, to simplify enrollment processes, and to coordinate existing coverage programs for children. As of July 2000, 50 states and the District of Columbia have received Covering Kids project grants. In general, states are

---

14, 1997. p. 26545-26550.
[46] CRS tabulations of Form HCFA-21C data.

not the recipients of these grants. Instead, the program provides grants to coalitions of community groups that will administer and implement the outreach and enrollment activities. While RWJF has not yet published an official tabulation of the specific outreach and enrollment strategies implemented by grantees across the country, the Covering Kids website [http://www.coveringkids.org] provides a variety of resources on these topics.

Legislative Changes to Major Outreach and Eligibility Provisions Under Medicaid and SCHIP

President Clinton's FY2001 budget included several initiatives that would have affected the Medicaid and SCHIP programs.[47] The 106th Congress made changes in line with some of the Clinton Administration's proposals (summarized below). The subset of the Clinton Administration's proposals aimed primarily at improving coverage for families and children would have: (1) replaced SCHIP with a new FamilyCare Program that would have provided health insurance to parents of children enrolled in Medicaid or SCHIP, and included financial incentives to cover whole families at higher income levels, (2) expanded Medicaid and SCHIP eligibility to 19- and 20-year-olds at state option,[48] (3) restored the option to provide full Medicaid eligibility to immigrants who lost coverage under welfare reform (including pregnant women, children and disabled immigrants regardless of date of entry into the US), (4) allowed states to use SCHIP funds to cover immigrant children, and (5) made transitional Medicaid coverage permanent and simplified state and family requirements to promote enrollment. In addition to these eligibility proposals, new outreach initiatives proposed by the Clinton Administration would have: (1) allowed School Lunch Programs to share participant information with Medicaid, (2) expanded sites authorized to presumptively enroll children in Medicaid and SCHIP to include schools, child care resource and referral centers, homeless programs, and other sites,

---

[47] These proposals are outlined in *Clinton-Gore Administration Unveils Major New Health Insurance Initiative* (January 19, 2000). CBO provides a detailed analysis of these proposals and alternative budget estimates in *An Analysis of the President's Budgetary Proposals for Fiscal Year 2001* (April 2000).

[48] Under current law, individuals who are 19 or 20 years of age can qualify for Medicaid if they are pregnant, disabled or meet welfare-related standards (i.e., are adults with dependent children). Some individuals in this age group who were formerly in foster care are also eligible for Medicaid. SCHIP eligibility is limited to those under 19 years of age.

and (3) required states to institute under Medicaid the same simplified enrollment procedures as those used under SCHIP.

Several bills were introduced in the 106th Congress that would have extended eligibility or facilitated continuous coverage, broadened outreach, simplified enrollment processes, and/or changed funding for such activities under Medicaid and SCHIP. Four such pieces of legislation were passed by the 106th Congress and signed into law. The first was the *Medicare, Medicaid, and SCHIP Balanced Budget Refinement Act of 1999* (BBRA 99; H.R. 3426) included by reference in the *Consolidated Appropriations Act for FY2000* (H.R. 3194) that became Public Law 106-113. Among other Medicaid provisions, this law permanently extended the availability of the $500 million Medicaid fund established to assist with the administrative costs of new Medicaid eligibility activities resulting from welfare reform. Second, the *Foster Care Independence Act of 1999* (P.L. 106-169) gave states the option to extend Medicaid coverage to former foster care recipients between 18 and 20 years of age.

In a move to eliminate a barrier posed by the Agriculture Department's former policy guidance, the *Agriculture Risk Protection Act* (H.R. 2559, P.L. 106-224) now permits schools to share income and other relevant information when determining eligibility for free or reduced-price meals in the School Lunch Program with state Medicaid and SCHIP agencies for the purpose of identifying and enrolling children in these two programs. This law also established a one-state pilot project under which administrative funds for the WIC program can be used to help identify and enroll eligible children in Medicaid and SCHIP.

The most far reaching piece of legislation was the *Medicare, Medicaid, and SCHIP Benefits Improvement and Protection Act of 2000* (BIPA; H.R. 4557) that became P.L. 106-554. This law made several important changes affecting eligibility, outreach and enrollment under Medicaid and SCHIP.

With respect to Medicaid, P.L. 106-554 extended by 1 year (to September 30, 2002) the availability of transitional medical assistance for families no longer eligible for Medicaid on the basis of meeting former AFDC rules. It also added several entities to the list of those qualified to make Medicaid presumptive eligibility determinations for children, including for example, schools, child support enforcement agencies, certain programs for the homeless, and federally funded housing assistance programs. (Prior Medicaid law defined qualified entities to include Medicaid providers, Head Start programs, WIC programs, and agencies that determine eligibility for subsidized child care.) In addition, a technical amendment in this law exempted from a general upper income limit rule those adolescents aging out of foster care who are eligible for Medicaid under the Foster Care Independence Act of 1999 (as well as certain women eligible for Medicaid under the Breast and Cervical Cancer Treatment Act of 2000).

Significant changes were also made to SCHIP under P.L. 106-554. Prior law required that unused SCHIP funds be redistributed only to those states that spend their full allotments for a given fiscal year within a specified time frame. P.L. 106-554 extends the availability of unused funds from FY1998 and FY999 (through the end of FY2002) and redistributes these unused funds among both those states that spend and those that do not spend their full original allotments for these years. As previously described, P.L. 106-554 also permits certain states to use up to 10% of retained FY1998 funds for outreach activities. Finally, the new law clarifies states' authority to conduct presumptive eligibility determinations, as defined in Medicaid law, under separate (non-Medicaid) SCHIP programs.

CONCLUSIONS

Recent trends in insurance coverage among children (and others) have shown some improvements. Expansions of eligibility under Medicaid in the last two decades, and the advent of SCHIP in late 1997, have significantly increased the opportunities for coverage among poor and near poor children. HCFA reported continued increases in SCHIP enrollment in FY1999, rising to 3.3 million children during FY2000. Other data for 1998 and 1999 suggest that the decline in Medicaid caseloads that began in the mid-1990s may have started to reverse itself. Despite these improved opportunities, there were an estimated 6.7 million low-income children eligible for, but not enrolled in either of these two programs in 1999. These enrollment patterns are affected by complex interactions between economic trends, federal and state policies, program administrative procedures, and beneficiary perceptions. These interactions result in considerable enrollment variability across states, suggesting that at least some solutions will need to be state-specific.

Under both Medicaid and SCHIP, states face a number of challenges in reaching and enrolling the current target populations, most notably the working poor and nearpoor, two-parent families, and immigrants. Medicaid faces the additional challenge of preventing previously enrolled individuals who remain eligible from dropping out of the program. Retention issues are beginning to surface under SCHIP as well.

Some policy makers have argued that providing Medicaid and SCHIP to whole families may be a more effective mechanism for reducing the number of low-income children without health insurance than the current fractured program structure. In recent years, able-bodied adults, typically parents of eligible children, experienced severe enrollment losses under Medicaid. Some of this loss was inadvertent, but the fact remains that there are few eligibility pathways into Medicaid, and even more restrictions under SCHIP, for providing coverage to low-income adults with children. Further simplification of eligibility rules, streamlining of enrollment processes and additional outreach are also important to reducing the number of low-income, uninsured children. Recent progress in these areas may be starting to take hold.

State budget limitations under Medicaid and SCHIP require state administrators to think carefully about their choice of outreach strategies and enrollment facilitation efforts. Cost-effectiveness should be a key consideration in making these choices. The existing research literature does not adequately pinpoint such strategies, but future evaluations at the state and federal level may fill this information gap. States may require a large investment of both time and money to evaluate the effectiveness of their outreach methods and enrollment simplification procedures, and to subsequently apply those lessons to their Medicaid and SCHIP programs.

SCHIP and Medicaid generally received continuing support from the 106th Congress. However, in recent months, there have been some signs that the economic growth enjoyed for the past several years may be slowing down. An economic downturn may increase the number of individuals eligible for Medicaid and SCHIP. Current SCHIP funding levels can probably absorb some of such an increase, but a huge influx of new enrollees into Medicaid could severely strain both federal and state budgets as was the case in the early to mid-1990s when major Medicaid reform was considered. If an economic downturn takes place, the 107th Congress may be faced with difficult domestic policy and funding choices. The goal of reducing the number of children without health insurance must be balanced with budget constraints that may result from any future economic downturns.

Table 1. Income Eligibility Standards for Medicaid and SCHIP (By Percentage of the Federal Poverty Level)

State[a]	Medicaid standards in effect 3/31/97[b] (lower income boundary for SCHIP)				Medicaid SCHIP-expansion program approved as of 12/11/00[c]	Separate SCHIP approved as of 12/11/00[c]
	Age 0 to 1	Ages 1 thru 5	Ages 6 thru 14	Ages 15 thru 18		
Alabama	133%	133%	100%	15%	100% (ages 17 thru 18)	200% (ages 0 thru 18)
Alaska	133%	133%	100%	100%	200% (ages 0 thru 18)	n/a
Arizona	140%	133%	100%	30%	n/a	200% (ages 0 thru 18)
Arkansas[d]	133%	133%	100%	18%	100% (born after 9/30/82 and before 10/1/83)	n/a
California	200%	133%	100%	82%	100% (ages 17 and 18)	250% (ages 0 thru 18)
Colorado	133%	133%	100%	37%	n/a	185% (ages 0 thru 18)
Connecticut	185%	185%	185%	100%	185% (ages 17 and 18)	300% (ages 0 thru 18)
Delaware	133%	133%	100%	100%	n/a	200% (ages 0 thru 18)
District of Columbia	185%	133%	100%	50%	200% (ages 0 thru 18)	n/a
Florida[e]	185%	133%	100%	28%	100% (ages 17 and 18) 200% (ages 0 thru 1)	200% (ages 1 thru 18)
Georgia	185%	133%	100%	100%	n/a	200% (ages 0 thru 18)
Hawaii	185%	133%	100%	100%	200% (ages 0 thru 18)	n/a
Idaho	133%	133%	100%	100%	150% (ages 0 thru 18)	n/a
Illinois	133%	133%	100%	46%	133% (ages 6 thru 18)	185% (ages 1 thru 18)
Indiana	150%	133%	100%	100%	150% (ages 1 thru 18)	200% (ages 0 thru 18)
Iowa	185%	133%	100%	37%	133% (ages 6 thru 18)	200% (ages 0 thru 18)
Kansas	150%	133%	100%	100%	n/a	200% (ages 0 thru 18)
Kentucky	185%	133%	100%	33%	150% (ages 1 thru 18)	200% (ages 0 thru 18)
Louisiana	133%	133%	100%	10%	150% (ages 0 thru 18)	n/a

Reaching Low-Income, Uninsured Children 115

State[a]	Medicaid standards in effect 3/31/97[b] (lower income boundary for SCHIP)				Medicaid SCHIP-expansion program approved as of 12/11/00[c]	Separate SCHIP approved as of 12/11/00[c]
	Age 0 to 1	Ages 1 thru 5	Ages 6 thru 14	Ages 15 thru 18		
Maine	185%	133%	125%	125%	150% (ages 1 thru 18)	185% (ages 1 thru 18)
Maryland	185%	185%	185%	100%	200% (ages 0 thru 18)	300%[f] (ages 0 thru 18)
Massachusetts	185%	133%	114%	86%	150% (ages 1 thru 18) 200% (ages 0 thru 1 and pregnant teens)	200% (ages 1 thru 18)
Michigan	185%	133%	100%	100%	150% (ages 17 and 18)	200% (ages 0 thru 18)
Minnesota	275%	275%	275%	275%	280% (below age 2)	n/a
Mississippi	185%	133%	100%	34%	100% (ages 17 and 18)	200% (ages 0 thru 18)
Missouri	185%	133%	100%	100%	300% (ages 0 thru 18)	n/a
Montana	133%	133%	100%	40.5%	n/a	150% (ages 0 thru 18)
Nebraska	150%	133%	100%	33%	185% (ages 0 thru 18)	n/a
Nevada	133%	133%	100%	31%	n/a	200% (ages 0 thru 18)
New Hampshire	185%	185%	185%	185%	300% (ages 0 thru 1)	300% (ages 1 thru 18)
New Jersey	185%	133%	100%	41%	133% (ages 6 thru 18)	350% (ages 0 thru 18)
New Mexico	185%	185%	185%	185%	235% (ages 0 thru 18)	n/a
New York[e]	185%	133%	100%	51%	100% (ages 17 and 18)	192% (ages 0 thru 18)
North Carolina	185%	133%	100%	100%	n/a	200% (ages 0 thru 18)
North Dakota	133%	133%	100%	100% (thru age 17)	100% (18 year olds)	140% (ages 0 thru 18)
Ohio	133%	133%	100%	33%	200% (ages 0 thru 18)	n/a
Oklahoma	150%	133%	100%	48%	185% (thru age 17)	n/a
Oregon	133%	133%	100%	100%	n/a	170% (ages 0 thru 18)
Pennsylvania[e]	185%	133%	100%	41%	n/a	200% (ages 0 thru 18)

State[a]	Medicaid standards in effect 3/31/97[b] (lower income boundary for SCHIP)				Medicaid SCHIP-expansion program approved as of 12/11/00[c]	Separate SCHIP approved as of 12/11/00[c]
	Age 0 to 1	Ages 1 thru 5	Ages 6 thru 14	Ages 15 thru 18		
Rhode Island[g]	250%	250% (thru age 7)	100% (ages 8 thru 14)	100%	250% (ages 8 thru 18)	n/a
South Carolina	185%	133%	100%	48%	150% (ages 1 thru 18)	n/a
South Dakota	133%	133%	100%	100%	140% (ages 0 thru 18)	200% (ages 0 thru 18)
Tennessee[h]	--	--	--	16%	100% (ages 17 and 18)	n/a
Texas	185%	133%	100%	17%	100% (ages 17 and 18)	200% (ages 0 thru 18)
Utah	133%	133%	100%	100% (thru age 17)	n/a	200% (ages 0 thru 18)
Vermont	225%	225%	225%	225%	n/a	300% (ages 0 thru 17)
Virginia	133%	133%	100%	100%	n/a	185% (ages 0 thru 18)
Washington	200%	200%	200%	200%	n/a	250% (ages 0 thru 18)
West Virginia	150%	133%	100%	100%	n/a	200% (ages 0 thru 18)
Wisconsin	185%	185%	100%	45%	185% (ages 6 thru 18)	n/a
Wyoming	133%	133%	100%	55%	n/a	133% (ages 6 thru 18)

Source: Health Care Financing Administration. *The State Children's Health Insurance Program, Annual Enrollment Report, October 1, 1998-September 30, 1999.* Baltimore, Health Care Financing Administration, January 11, 2000. Medicaid expansion and separate state expansion program eligibility limits were updated to reflect amendments approved as of 12/11/00.

[a] The Territories are not included in this table. Due to the unique nature of their SCHIP plans, the U.S. Territories and jurisdictions may cover existing Medicaid populations with SCHIP funds, but only after their Medicaid funding caps are reached.

[b] SCHIP contains a provision that a child's family income must exceed the Medicaid income level that was in effect on March 31, 1997 in order for that child to be eligible for SCHIP-funded coverage. If approved, the proposed rule (published in the *Federal Register*, v. 64, no. 215, Monday, November 8, 1999) will change that date from March 31, 1997 to June 1, 1997 — a change that will affect the eligibility in a few states. On January 5, 2001, the Department of Health and Human Services released the final rule implementing comprehensive program requirements and administrative procedures for SCHIP. The final SCHIP rule is scheduled to be published in the January 11, 2001 *Federal Register* and will become effective 90 days after publication.

[c] Reflects upper eligibility level of SCHIP plans and amendments approved as of December 11, 2000. Upper eligibility is defined as a percent of the federal poverty level (FPL), which, in 1999, is $16,700 for a family of 4. In general, states with Medicaid expansion SCHIP

programs must establish their upper eligibility levels net of income disregards. States with separate SCHIP programs can establish their upper eligibility levels on a gross income basis or net of income disregards.

[d] Arkansas increased Medicaid eligibility to 200% FPL effective September 1997 though section 1115 demonstration authority.

[e] These states had state-funded programs that existed prior to SCHIP. Title XXI permitted children previously in these state-funded programs to be covered under SCHIP and requires these states to maintain their previous level of state spending.

[f] Maryland's Expansion to 300% was approved but will be implemented on July 1, 2001.

[g] Rhode Island has implemented its program to 250% of the FPL. The state also has an approved amendment (February 5, 1999) in place to further expand the program to 300% of the FPL.

[h] Under its section 1115 demonstration, Tennessee has no upper eligibility level. The currently approved SCHIP plan covers children born before October 1, 1983 in the expansion group and who enrolled in TennCare on or after April 1, 1997.

Table 2. National Medicaid Enrollment Levels, FY1995-FY1998

Type of beneficiary	Enrollment levels (thousands)				Percent change			
	FY1995	FY1996	FY1997	FY1998	1995-1996	1996-1997	1997-1998	1995-1998
Adults	9,600	9,255	8,583	8,643	-3.6	-7.3	0.7	-10.0
Cash related	5,399	4,934	4,082	3,452	-8.6	-17.3	-15.4	-36.1
Other	4,202	4,321	4,501	5,190	2.8	4.2	15.3	23.5
Children	21,630	21,259	21,058	20,665	-1.7	-0.9	-1.9	-4.5
Cash related	11,236	10,474	8,931	7,640	-6.8	-14.7	-14.5	-32.0
Other	10,393	10,785	12,127	13,025	3.8	12.4	7.4	25.3
Aged	4,115	4,117	4,114	4,090	0.0	-0.1	-0.6	-0.6
Cash related	1,847	1,840	1,813	1,783	-0.4	-1.5	-1.7	-3.5
Other	2,268	2,278	2,301	2,306	0.4	1.0	0.2	1.7
Disabled	6,333	6,664	6,836	6,984	5.2	2.6	2.2	10.3
Cash related	5,025	5,268	5,331	5,448	4.8	1.2	2.2	8.4
Other	1,308	1,396	1,505	1,536	6.7	7.8	2.1	17.4
Total Medicaid	**41,677**	**41,295**	**40,591**	**40,381**	**-0.9**	**-1.7**	**-0.5**	**-3.1**

Source: Unpublished Urban Institute (UI) estimates based on data from HCFA 2082-reports (12/14/00). Percent change calculations estimated by the Congressional Research Service (CRS). Does not include the U.S. Territories. Figures may not sum to totals due to rounding. Enrollees are defined as people who sign up for Medicaid for any length of time in a given fiscal year. Due to variations in the duration of enrollment periods, the reported number of enrollees tends to be higher than point-in-time estimates and the enrollment distributions may differ substantially from those based on point-in-time estimates. "Cash related" refers to enrollees who receive AFDC (prior to welfare reform), SSI, or mandatory state cash supplements, or who qualify for Medicaid via old AFDC rules (after welfare reform). "Other" includes all other enrollees, primarily the medically needy, poverty-related expansion groups, and people eligible under Medicaid Section 1115 waivers. Some states may include Title XXI program (SCHIP) enrollees in their HCFA-2082 forms, though this should not be the case.

Note: For data quality reasons, we elected to summarize UI's analysis in this report, rather than official HCFA-2082 data (named for the label on the reporting form). States generate 2082 data from their Medicaid administrative files using a standard format accompanied by instructions from HCFA. Historically, these official data have contained some classification errors and missing information. The magnitude of these problems varies by state and fiscal year. UI edited HCFA's 2082 data to minimize these data problems. In particular, for the analysis summarized here, UI reassigned cases classified as "unknown" or "other" for basis of eligibility into the adult, children, aged and disabled categories. UI replaced missing data when possible. Other state- and year-specific edits were also performed. To inform this editing process and derive alternative counts, they performed distributional analysis on other 2082 data elements, contacted state officials to identify appropriate adjustments, and substituted other state data when available. Thus, UI's numbers do not match official HCFA data for fiscal years 1995 through 1998.

Table 3. Selected Enrollment, Verification and Redetermination Strategies for Children Under Medicaid and SCHIP, July 2000

Selected strategies	Medicaid (50 states and the District of Columbia)	Separate SCHIP programs (32 states)
Simplification criteria at initial application		
Joint application for Medicaid and SCHIP	N/A[a]	28 (87.5%)
No face-to-face interview	40 (78.4%)	31 (96.9%)
No asset test	42 (82.4%)	31 (96.9%)
Presumptive eligibility[b]	8 (15.7%)	4 (12.5%)
12-months continuous eligibility[c]	14 (27.4%)	22 (68.8%)
Self-declaration of income as verification[d]	10 (19.6%)	7 (21.9%)
Redetermination procedures		
Joint application for Medicaid and SCHIP	N/A[a]	14 (43.7%)
No face-to-face interview	43 (84.3%)	32 (100%)

Source: Ross, D., and Cox, L. Making It Simple: Medicaid for Children and CHIP Income Eligibility Guidelines and Enrollment Procedures: Findings from a 50-State Survey. Washington, D.C., The Kaiser Commission on Medicaid and the Uninsured, October 2000.

Note: The "Medicaid" column indicates the number of states that have adopted a particular strategy for their children's Medicaid program. It includes all 50 state Medicaid programs and the District of Columbia, regardless of whether the state implemented a Medicaid expansion, a separate SCHIP program, or a combination of the two, with its SCHIP allotment.

The "Separate SCHIP Programs" column indicates the number of states that have adopted a particular strategy for their SCHIP-funded, separate state program. It includes 32 states (AL, AZ, CA, CO, CT, DE, FL, GA, IL IN, IA, KS, KY, ME, MA, MI, MS, MT, NV, NH, NJ, NY, NC, ND, OR, PA, TX, UT, VA, WA, WV, and WY). The remaining 19 states have chosen to use their SCHIP allotment to expand Medicaid exclusively and are not included in this column.

[a] A joint application for Medicaid and SCHIP is only relevant in the 32 states that have both Medicaid and separate SCHIP programs. See column 3.

[b] Presumptive eligibility allows children whose family income appears to be below the state's Medicaid income-eligibility guidelines to enroll temporarily in Medicaid, giving families time to complete the formal application process. While several states have adopted a presumptive eligibility procedure for their separate SCHIP programs, the rules under the Medicaid presumptive eligibility option do not necessarily apply.

[c] States have the option to continuously enroll children in Medicaid for up to 12 months, without regard to changes in their family income. Families are not obliged to report changes in their circumstances that may occur before the end of the 12-month enrollment period. This option applies for both initial enrollment and redetermination periods. The states reporting 12 months of continuous eligibility at initial application also provide 12-month redetermination periods.

[d] Federal Medicaid rules require states to verify information on the application form through various data exchanges with other agencies (for example, the Social Security Administration and the state agency that administers unemployment insurance). Federal law, however, does not require families to supply third-party verification of information provided in the application, except in one situation – when the person seeking coverage is not a citizen, documentation of the non-citizen's immigration status is required. Otherwise, states have the flexibility to determine documentation requirements and can allow self-declaration of income.

Chapter 4

STATE CHILDREN'S HEALTH INSURANCE PROGRAM: A BRIEF OVERVIEW[†]

Elicia J. Herz and Peter Kraut

The Balanced Budget Act of 1997 (BBA 97; P.L. 105-33) established the State Children's Health Insurance Program (SCHIP) under a new Title XXI of the Social Security Act. In general, the program offers federal matching funds to states and territories to provide health insurance to certain low-income children.

ELIGIBILITY

Under SCHIP, states may cover children in families with incomes that are above the state's Medicaid eligibility standard but less than 200% of the federal poverty level (FPL).[1] However, states in which the maximum Medicaid income level for children was at or above 200% FPL prior to the enactment of SCHIP may increase this income level by an additional 50 percentage points above the level used under the state's Medicaid program.

[†] Excerpted from CRS Report RL30473.
[1] For example, in 2001, the poverty guideline in the 48 contiguous states and the District of Columbia was $17,650 for a family of four (see *the Federal Register*, v. 66, no. 33, February 16, 2001. p. 10695-10697.)

Not all targeted low-income children will necessarily receive medical assistance under SCHIP for two reasons. First, unlike Medicaid, federal law does not establish an *individual* entitlement[2] to benefits under SCHIP. Instead, it entitles *states* with approved SCHIP plans to pre-determined federal allotments based on a distribution formula set in the law. Second, each state can define the group of targeted low-income children who may enroll in SCHIP. Title XXI allows states to use the following factors in determining eligibility: geography, age, income and resources, residency, disability status (so long as any standard relating to that status does not restrict eligibility), and access to other health insurance. Title XXI funds cannot be used for children who would have been eligible for the state's Medicaid plan under the eligibility standards that were in effect prior to the enactment of the law establishing SCHIP or for children covered by a group health plan or other insurance.

As of September, 2000, the upper income eligibility limit under SCHIP had reached 350% of the FPL (see **Table 1**).[3] Nearly one-half (23) of the states had established upper income limits at 200% FPL. Another 10 states exceeded 200% FPL. The remaining 18 states set maximum income levels below 200% FPL. Ten states had asset tests for some groups of children, typically those in Medicaid rather than separate state programs (see Benefits subsection).[4]

---

[2] The one exception to this rule is when a state chooses to implement a Medicaid expansion under SCHIP. Children who qualify for SCHIP through a Medicaid expansion are entitled to Medicaid benefits as long as they continue to meet these specific eligibility criteria (even if SCHIP itself terminates) or until the state is granted approval to eliminate the eligibility category created by the Medicaid expansion through SCHIP.

[3] For determining income eligibility for SCHIP and Medicaid, some states apply "income disregards." These are specified dollar amounts subtracted from gross income to compute net income, which is then compared to the applicable income criterion. Such disregards *increase* the *effective* income level above the stated standard. State SCHIP plans do not consistently report the use of income disregards, nor whether the stated income standards include or exclude such disregards.

[4] States may apply resource or asset tests in determining financial eligibility, but are not required to do so. Individuals must have resources for which the dollar value is less than a specified standard amount in order to qualify for coverage. States determine what items constitute countable resources and the dollar value assigned to those countable resources. Assets may include, for example, cars, savings accounts, real estate, trust funds, tax credits, etc. See Ross, D., and Cox, L. *Making It Simple: Medicaid for Children and CHIP Income Eligibility Guidelines and Enrollment Procedures: Findings from a 50-State Survey.* Washington, D.C.: The Kaiser Commission on Medicaid and the Uninsured, October, 2000.

BENEFITS

States may choose from three options when designing their SCHIP programs. They may expand their current Medicaid program, create a new "separate state" insurance program, or devise a combination of both approaches. Under limited circumstances, states have the option to purchase a health benefits plan that is provided by a community-based health delivery system or to purchase family coverage under a group health plan as long as it is cost effective to do so.[5]

States that choose to expand Medicaid to new eligibles under SCHIP must provide the full range of mandatory Medicaid benefits, as well as all optional services specified in their state Medicaid plans. Alternately, states may choose any of three other benefit options: (1) a benchmark benefit package, (2) benchmark equivalent coverage, or (3) any other health benefits plan that the Secretary of Health and Human Services determines will provide appropriate coverage to the targeted population of uninsured children.[6]

A benchmark benefit package is one of the following three plans: (1) the standard Blue Cross/Blue Shield preferred provider option plan offered under the Federal Employees Health Benefits Program (FEHBP), (2) the health coverage that is offered and generally available to state employees in the state involved, and (3) the health coverage that is offered by a health maintenance organization (HMO) with the largest commercial (non-Medicaid) enrollment in the state involved.

Benchmark equivalent coverage is defined as a package of benefits that has the same actuarial value as one of the benchmark benefit packages. A state choosing to provide benchmark equivalent coverage must cover each of the benefits in the "basic benefits category." The benefits in the basic benefits category are inpatient and outpatient hospital services, physicians' surgical and medical services, lab and x-ray services, and well-baby and well-child care, including age-appropriate immunizations. Benchmark equivalent coverage must also include at least 75% of the actuarial value of

---

[5] In the case of community-based health delivery systems, the cost of coverage cannot exceed, on an average per child basis, the cost of coverage that would otherwise be provided. In the case of family coverage, the alternative must be cost-effective relative to the amount paid to obtain comparable coverage only of the targeted low-income children, and it must not substitute for health insurance coverage that would otherwise be provided to the children.

[6] When the law establishing SCHIP was enacted, existing state programs in Florida, New York, and Pennsylvania were designated as meeting the minimum benefit requirements under this program.

coverage under the benchmark plan for each of the benefits in the "additional service category." These additional services include prescription drugs, mental health services, vision services, and hearing services. States are encouraged to cover other categories of service not fisted above. Abortions may not be covered, except in the case of a pregnancy resulting from rape or incest, or when an abortion is necessary to save the mother's life.

COST-SHARING

Cost-sharing refers to the out-of-pocket payments made by beneficiaries of a health insurance plan. Cost-sharing may include, for example, monthly premiums, enrollment fees, deductibles, copayments, coinsurance and other similar charges.

Federal law permits states to impose cost-sharing for some beneficiaries and some services under SCHIP. States that choose to implement SCHIP as a Medicaid expansion must follow the nominal cost-sharing rules of the Medicaid program.

If a state implements SCHIP through a separate state program, premiums or enrollment fees for program participation may be imposed, but the maximum allowable amount is dependent on family income. For all families with incomes under 150% FPL and enrolled in separate state programs, premiums may not exceed the amounts set forth in federal Medicaid regulations. Additionally, these families may be charged service-related cost-sharing, but such cost-sharing is limited to (1) nominal amounts defined in federal Medicaid regulations for the subgroup with income below 100% FPL, and (2) slightly higher amounts defined in SCHIP regulations for families with income between 101-150% FPL. For a family with income above 150% FPL, cost-sharing may be imposed in any amount, provided that cost-sharing for higher income children is not less than cost-sharing for lower income children.

Most importantly, the total annual aggregate cost-sharing (including premiums, deductibles, copayments and any other charges) for all children in any SCHIP family may not exceed 5% of total family income for the year. In addition, states must inform families of these limits and provide a mechanism for families to stop paying once the cost-sharing limits have been reached.

Preventive services are exempt from cost-sharing for all families regardless of income. The Centers for Medicare and Medicaid Services

(CMS) defines preventive services to include the following: all healthy newborn inpatient physician visits, including routine screening (inpatient and outpatient); routine physical examinations; laboratory tests; immunizations and related office visits; and routine preventive and diagnostic dental services (for example, oral examinations, prophylaxis and topical fluoride applications, sealants, and x-rays).

FINANCING

BBA 97 appropriated a total of $39.7 billion for SCHIP for FY1998 through FY2007.[7] The funding level by fiscal year varies across time. The total annual appropriation for each of FY1998 through FY2001 is about $4.3 billion. This annual total drops to about $3.2 billion for FY2002 through FY2004, then rises to $4.1 billion for FY2005 and FY2006, with a further increase to $5.0 billion in FY2007.

Allotment of funds among the states is determined by a formula set in law. This formula is based on a combination of the number of low-income children and low-income, uninsured children in the state, and includes a cost factor that represents average wages in the state compared to the national average. A state with an approved plan has 3 fiscal years in which to draw down a given year's funding. Also, a state must draw down its entire allotment for a given fiscal year before it can access the next year's funding.

Like Medicaid, SCHIP is a federal-state matching program. For each dollar of state spending, the federal government makes a matching payment. A state's share of program spending is equal to 100% minus the enhanced federal medical assistance percentage (FMAP). The enhanced SCHIP FMAP is equal to a state's Medicaid FMAP increased by the number of percentage points that is equal to 30% multiplied by the number of percentage points by which the FMAP is less than 100%.[8] For example, among states with a Medicaid FMAP of 60%, under Medicaid such states must spend 40 cents

---

[7] The law sets aside 0.25% of SCHIP funds for five territories and commonwealths (Puerto Rico, Guam, Virgin Islands, American Samoa, and the Northern Mariana Islands). It also sets aside $60 million annually for Special Diabetes Grants for FY1998 through FY2002 only.

[8] The federal medical assistance percentage (FMAP) and the enhanced federal medical assistance percentage (enhanced FMAP) are calculated and published annually by the Secretary of DHHS. FMAP is a measure of the average income per person in each state, squared, compared to that of the nation as a whole. This formula is designed to provide a higher FMAP to states with lower per capita income.

for every 60 cents that the federal government contributes. The enhanced FMAP for such states equals the Medicaid FMAP increased by 12 percentage points (60%+[30% multiplied by 40 percentage points]=72%.) In this example, the state share equals 100%-72%=28%.

Compared with the Medicaid FMAP, which ranges from 50% to 76.09% in FY2002, the enhanced FMAP for SCHIP ranges from 65% to 83.26%. All SCHIP assistance for targeted tow-income children, including child health coverage provided through a Medicaid expansion, is eligible for the enhanced FMAP. The Medicaid FMAP and the enhanced SCHIP FMAP are subject to a ceiling of 83% and 85%, respectively.

There is a limit on federal spending for SCHIP administrative expenses, which include activities such as data collection and reporting, as well as outreach and education. For federal matching purposes, a 10% cap applies to state administrative expenses. This cap is tied to the dollar amount that a state draws down from its annual allotment to cover benefits under SCHIP, as opposed to 10% of a state's total annual allotment.

LEGISLATIVE HISTORY

Under BBA 97, the State Children's Health Insurance Program was established, effective August 5, 1997. A number of provisions specified eligibility criteria; coverage requirements for health insurance; federal allotments and the state allocation formula; payments to states and the enhanced FMAP formula; the process for submission, approval and amendment of state SCHIP plans; strategic objectives and performance goals, and plan administration; annual reports and evaluations; options for expanding coverage of children under Medicaid; and diabetes grant programs.

During late 1997 through December of 2001, changes to SCHIP have been included in five laws passed subsequent to BBA 97. Major provisions affecting SCHIP in these laws are summarized below.

The District of Columbia Appropriations Act of 1998 (P.L. 105-100) and the 1998 Supplemental Appropriations and Rescissions Act (P.L. 105-174) made technical corrections to SCHIP. In addition, P.L. 105-100 increased the FY1998 SCHIP appropriation from $4.275 billion to $4.295 billion.

Two changes to SCHIP were made in the Omnibus Consolidated and Emergency Supplemental Appropriation Act, FY1999 (P.L. 105-277). For

FY1999, an additional appropriation of $32 million for the territories was provided, bringing the FY1999 total appropriation to $4.295 billion. In addition, for FY1998 and FY1999, this law changed the annual state allotment formula by stipulating that children with access to health care funded by the Indian Health Service and no other health insurance would be counted as uninsured (rather than as insured as required under the previously existing law).

The Medicare, Medicaid and SCHIP Balanced Budget Refinement Act of 1999 (BBRA 99; incorporated by reference in P.L. 106-113) made a number of mostly technical corrections to the program, of which the major changes are enumerated below:[9]

1. *Stabilizing the SCHIP allotment formula* - Annual federal allotments to each state are determined in part by states' success in covering previously uninsured low-income children under SCHIP. Under prior law, the more successful a state was in enrolling children in SCHIP, especially early in the program, the greater the potential reduction in subsequent annual allotments. To limit the amount a state's allocation can fluctuate from one year to the next, BBRA 99 modified the allotment distribution formula and established new floors and ceilings.

2. *Targeted, increased allotments* - Additional allotments for the commonwealths and territories were provided for fiscal years 2000 through 2007.

3. *Improved data collection and evaluation* - First, the law provided new funding for the collection of data to produce reliable, annual state-level estimates of the number of uninsured children. These data changes will improve research and evaluation efforts. They will also affect state-specific counts of the number of low-income children and the number of such children who are uninsured that feed into the formula that determines annual state-specific allotments from federal SCHIP appropriations. Second, new funding was also provided for a federal evaluation to identify

---

[9] For a detailed comparison of prior law and changes to SCHIP under BBRA 99, see CRS Report RL30400, *Medicaid and the State Children's Health Insurance Program (SCHIP): Provisions in the Consolidated Appropriations Act for FY2000*, by Jean Hearne and Elicia Herz.

effective outreach and enrollment practices for both SCHIP and Medicaid, barriers to enrollment, and factors influencing beneficiary drop-out. Finally, the law also required: (a) an inspector general audit and GAO report on enrollment of Medicaid-eligible children in SCHIP, (b) states to report annually the number of deliveries to pregnant women and the number of infants who receive services under the Maternal and Child Health Services Block Grant or who are entitled to SCHIP benefits, and (c) the Secretary of Health and Human Services to establish a clearinghouse for the consolidation and coordination of all federal databases and reports regarding children's health.

Finally, the Medicare, Medicaid and SCHIP Benefits Improvement and Protection Act of 2000 (BIPA), incorporated by reference into P.L. 106-554, included three major changes to SCHIP:[10]

1. *Special redistribution rules for unspent FY1998 and FY1999 allotments* - At the end of the 3-year period of availability, unspent allotments for a given fiscal year are subject to redistribution among only those states that fully expend their allotments, by a method to be determined by the Secretary of Health and Human Services. States had until the end of FY2000 to spend their FY1998 allotments. Similarly, FY1999 allotments had to be spent by the end of FY2001. BIPA established special redistribution rules for unspent FY1998 and FY1999 allotments. First, states that fully expended their original allotments for each of these years will receive redistributed amounts equal to their excess spending.[11] Then, the states that did not use all their original allotments for these years will retain a proportion of the remaining unspent funds. This proportion is the ratio of such a state's unspent original allotment to the total amount of unspent funds for that fiscal year. These latter states are permitted to use up to 10% of their retained FY1998 funds for outreach activities. This allowance is over and

---

[10] For other changes to Medicaid and SCHIP under BIPA, see CRS Report RL30718, *Medicaid, SCHIP and Other Health Provisions in H.R. 5661: Medicare, Medicaid and SCHIP Benefits Improvement and Protection Act of 2000,* by Jean Hearne, Elicia Herz and Evelyne Baumrucker.

[11] Each territory that spends its original allotment for these fiscal years will receive an amount that bears the same ratio to 1.05% of the total amount available for redistribution as the ratio of its original allotment bears to the total allotment for all territories.

above spending for such activities under the general administrative cap described above. All redistributed and retained funds from FY1998 and FY1999 must be spent by the end of FY2002.

2. *Presumptive eligibility* - Under Medicaid presumptive eligibility rules, states are allowed to temporarily enroll children whose family income appears to be below Medicaid income standards, until a final formal determination of eligibility is made. BIPA clarified states' authority to conduct presumptive eligibility determinations, as defined in Medicaid law, under separate (non-Medicaid) SCHIP programs.

3. *Authority to pay SCHIP Medicaid expansion costs from Title XXI appropriation* - Under prior law, states' allotments under SCHIP paid only the federal share of costs associated with separate (non-Medicaid) SCHIP programs. The federal share of costs associated with SCHIP Medicaid expansions were paid for under Medicaid. State SCHIP allotments were reduced by the amounts paid under Medicaid for SCHIP Medicaid expansion costs. BIPA authorized the payment of the costs of SCHIP Medicaid expansions and the costs of benefits provided during periods of presumptive eligibility from the SCHIP appropriation rather than the Medicaid appropriation, and as a conforming amendment, eliminated the requirement that state SCHIP allotments be reduced by these (former) Medicaid payments. Also, for FY1998-FY2000 only, BIPA authorized the transfer of unexpended SCHIP appropriations to the Medicaid appropriation account for the purpose of reimbursing payments associated with SCHIP Medicaid expansion programs.

PROGRAM DATA

The 50 states, the District of Columbia and five territories operate 56 SCHIP programs. As of early January 2002, 21 are Medicaid expansions, 16 are separate state programs, and 19 provide health insurance coverage through a combination approach.

Also as of early January, 2002, 99 amendments to original state plans had been approved and 10 more were in review. Several states have multiple amendments. The content of the plan amendments varies among states. For example, some states use the amendments to extend coverage beyond income levels defined in their original state plans. Others define new copayment standards for program participants. Still others modify benefit packages.

In addition to the amendment process, states that want to make changes to their SCHIP programs that go beyond what the law will allow may do so through what is called an 1115 waiver (named for the section of the Social Security Act that defines the circumstances under which such waivers may be granted). The Secretary of Health and Human Services may waive certain statutory requirements for conducting research and demonstration projects under SCHIP that allow states to adapt their programs to specific needs. As of late December, 2001, CMS had approved five such 1115 waivers (nine other waivers are in review). Four states will extend coverage to certain low-income parents, and two of these four states will also cover certain pregnant women. A fifth state will modify its cost-sharing rules for SCHIP Medicaid expansion participants.

On August 4, 2001, the Bush Administration announced the Health Insurance Flexibility and Accountability (HIFA) Demonstration Initiative. Using 1115 waiver authority, this initiative is designed to encourage states to extend Medicaid and SCHIP to the uninsured, with a particular emphasis on statewide approaches that maximize private health insurance coverage options and target populations with income below 200% FPL. Arizona is the first state to apply for a HIFA waiver, submitted in September. This proposal will expand SCHIP coverage to parents and certain childless and single adults.

Early enrollment estimates indicated that nearly 1 million children (982,000) were enrolled in SCHIP under 43 operational state programs as of December 1998.[12] Nearly 2 million children (1,979,450) were enrolled in SCHIP during FY1999 under 53 operational state programs.[13] The latest official numbers show that total SCHIP enrollment reached 3.3 million children in FY2000 (see **Table** 1). Of this total, 2.3 million were covered in separate state programs, and just over 1 million participated in SCHIP Medicaid expansions.

---

[12] U.S. Health Care Financing Administration. *A Preliminary Estimate of the Children's Health Insurance Program Aggregate Enrollment Numbers Through December 31,1998* (background only). April 20, 1999.

[13] U.S. Health Care Financing Administration. *The State Children's Health Insurance Program, Annual Enrollment Report, October 1, 1998 - September 30, 1999* (no date).

As described above, states and territories are provided annual federal SCHIP allotments based on a distribution formula set in law. These annual allotments are basically separate, sequential funding accounts. For each state and territory, the account for a given fiscal year is made available at the beginning of that year, and remains available for up to 3 years. SCHIP payments are taken out of the earliest active account. Once that fiscal year allotment is fully expended, and the next year's allotment becomes available (active), states can begin to access the next fiscal year's allotment, and so forth.

The most recent state-level information available on cumulative SCHIP expenditures since program inception and active allotment accounts are through September 2001 (see Table 2). During this reporting period, 4 fiscal year accounts - FY1998 through FY2001 - were available to states.[14]

To date, spending has fallen well below allotment levels for a variety of reasons. Despite the fact that 42 states began their SCHIP programs in late 1997 or 1998 (see Table 1), new programs take time to get off the ground and participation rates have been lower than expected. Nineteen states had spent less than 25% of their available allotments through September, 2001. Of these nineteen states, five had spent less than 10% of these funds. Another twenty-two states had used between one-fourth and one-half of their allotments. Only ten states had expended more than 50% of available funds.

To better understand these spending patterns it is necessary to look at specific fiscal year account activity by state. FY1998 represents a unique circumstance. Only 12 states[15] (and all 5 territories) had My expended their original allotments for this account by the end of FY2000 as required. These states and territories received redistributed funds as authorized by BIPA and described above. Alaska stands out as an exception in this group of 12 states. It exhausted all four available fiscal year accounts, as well as its redistributed FY1998 money. The remaining 11 states are either currently using or have exhausted their FY1999 or FY2000 allotment accounts. Some are spending

---

[14] Federal fiscal years run from October 1 through September 30 and are labeled according to the calendar year in which they end. So for example, the current fiscal year 2002 began on October 1, 2001 and will end on September 30, 2002. Under SCHIP, FY1998 funds were available through the end of FY2000 (September 30, 2000). FY1999 funds were available through the end of FY2001 (September 30, 2001). Unspent funds for these two fiscal years will be redistributed as authorized under BIPA (described above). FY2000 funds are available through FY2002, and FY2001 funds are available through FY2003.

[15] These 12 states, all marked with a # in Table 2, include Alaska, Indiana, Kentucky, Maine, Maryland, Massachusetts, Missouri, New York, North Carolina, Pennsylvania, Rhode Island, and South Carolina.

redistributed FY1998 funds which are available through FY2002, and others have not yet tapped into these additional funds.

The remaining 39 states (including the District of Columbia) did not spend their full FY1998 allotments by the end of FY2000. (As noted above, only 12 states did). However, these 39 states still received "retained" allotment amounts in the FY1998 redistribution process. As of September 2001, 14 of these 39 states were still accessing these retained allotments (see the FY1998 column in **Table** 2); 23 were accessing their FY1999 accounts, and 2 were accessing their FY2000 accounts. Redistribution of unspent FY1999 funds, as authorized under BIPA, has been determined by CMS, and will be based on the spending patterns shown in **Table** 2. Publication of the FY1999 redistribution/retention amounts by state is forthcoming.

Overall, most states have a long way to go to spend their currently available allotments. Nationally, through September 2001, 33% of available funds had been expended, leaving an unspent balance of approximately $11.3 billion from the FY1998 through FY2001 allotments. In October 2001, CMS published the final FY2002 allotment amounts.[16]

---

[16] State Children's Health Insurance Program; Final Allotments to States, the District of Columbia, and U.S. Territories and Commonwealth for Fiscal Year 2002, *Federal Register,* v. 66, DO. 208, October 26, 2001.

Table 1. State Children's Health Insurance Program (SCHIP) Aggregate Enrollment Statistics for the 50 States and the District of Columbia for Federal Fiscal Year (FFY) 2000[a]

State	Type of SCHIP program[b]	Date implemented	SCHIP upper income eligibility standard (%FPL)[c]	FFY 2000 enrollment (number of children ever enrolled during year)		
				Medicaid expansion	Separate child health program	Combined[d]
Alabama	Combination	02/01/98	200%	N/A	37,587	37,587
Alaska	Medicaid	03/01/99	200%	13,413		13,413
Arizona	Separate	11/01/98	200%		60,803	60,803
Arkansas	Medicaid	10/01/98	100%[e]	1,892		1,892
California	Combination	03/01/98	250%	48,974	428,641	477,615
Colorado	Separate	04/22/98	185%		34,889	34,889
Connecticut	Combination	07/01/98	300%	9,211	9,593	18,804
Delaware	Separate	02/01/99	200%		4,474	4,474
District of Columbia	Medicaid	10/01/98	200%	2,264[f]		2,264
Florida	Combination	04/01/98	200%	26,054	201,409	227,463
Georgia	Separate	11/01/98	200%		120,626	120,626
Hawaii	Medicaid	07/01/00	200%	2,256		2,256
Idaho	Medicaid	10/01/97	150%	12,449		12,449
Illinois	Combination	01/05/98	185%	44,848	17,659	62,507
Indiana	Combination	10/01/97	200%	44,373	N/A	44,373
Iowa	Combination	07/01/98	200%	11,259	8,699	19,958
Kansas	Separate	01/01/99	200%		26,306	26,306
Kentucky	Combination	07/01/98	200%	41,116	14,477	55,593
Louisiana	Medicaid	11/01/98	150%	49,995		49,995
Maine	Combination	07/01/98	185%[g]	13,914	8,828	22,742
Maryland	Medicaid[h]	07/01/98	200%[i]	93,081		93,081
Massachusetts	Combination	10/01/97	200%	72,906	40,128	113,034
Michigan	Combination	05/01/98	200%	15,917	21,231	37,148

State	Type of SCHIP program[b]	Date implemented	SCHIP upper income eligibility standard (%FPL)[c]	FFY 2000 enrollment (number of children ever enrolled during year)		Combined[d]
				Medicaid expansion	Separate child health program	
Minnesota	Medicaid	10/01/98	280%	24		24
Mississippi	Combination	07/01/98	200%	12,156	8,295[j]	20,451
Missouri	Medicaid	09/01/98	300%	73,825		73,825
Montana	Separate	01/01/99	150%		8,317	8,317
Nebraska	Medicaid	05/01/98	185%	11,400		11,400
Nevada	Separate	10/01/98	200%		15,946	15,946
New Hampshire	Combination	05/01/98	300%	153	4,119	4,272
New Jersey	Combination	03/01/98	350%	38,673	50,361	89,034
New Mexico	Medicaid	03/31/99	235%	6,106		6,106
New York	Combination	04/15/98	192%[k]	5,310	764,147	769,457
North Carolina	Separate	10/01/98	200%		103,567	103,567
North Dakota	Combination	10/01/98	140%	306	2,267	2,573
Ohio	Medicaid	01/01/98	200%	111,436		111,436
Oklahoma	Medicaid	12/01/97	185%	57,719		57,719
Oregon	Separate	07/01/98	170%		37,092	37,092
Pennsylvania	Separate	05/28/98	200%		119,710	119,710
Rhode Island	Medicaid	10/01/97	250%	11,539		11,539
South Carolina	Medicaid	10/01/97	150%	59,853		59,853
South Dakota	Combination	07/01/98	200%	5,589	299	5,888
Tennessee	Medicaid	10/01/97	100%[l]	14,861		14,861
Texas	Combination	07/01/98	200%	45,545	84,974	130,519
Utah	Separate	08/03/98	200%		25,294	25,294
Vermont	Separate	10/01/98	300%		4,081	4,081
Virginia	Separate	10/22/98	185%		37,681	37,681
Washington	Separate	02/01/00	250%		2,616	2,616
West Virginia	Combination[m]	07/01/98	150%[n]	3,243	18,416	21,659

State	Type of SCHIP program[b]	Date implemented	SCHIP upper income eligibility standard (%FPL)[c]	FFY 2000 enrollment (number of children ever enrolled during year)		
				Medicaid expansion	Separate child health program	Combined[d]
Wisconsin	Medicaid	04/01/99	185%	47,140		47,140
Wyoming	Separate	12/01/99	133%		2,547	2,547
National Totals				1,008,800	2,325,079	3,333,879

Source: Centers for Medicare and Medicaid Services website at [http://www.hcfa.gov/init/children.htm] (no date).

N/A = not available; FPL=federal poverty level.

[a] State-reported enrollment figures for SCHIP for October 1, 1999, through September 30, 2000. These figures do not include title XIX Medicaid enrollment

[b] Program type as of September 30, 2000.

[c] Upper eligibility standard approved and in effect as of September 30, 2000.

[d] For states with combination programs, mis column shows the sum of the unduplicated number of children ever enrolled in the Medicaid expansion program during the year and the unduplicated number of children ever enrolled in the separate child health program during the year. Because a child may be enrolled in both programs during the year, there may be some double counting of children enrolled in these states.

[e] Arkansas increased Medicaid eligibility to 200% of the FPL, effective September 1997, though a Medicaid section 1115 demonstration. Only children bora after September 30,1982 but before October 1, 1983, are eligible for SCHIP.

[f] Because the state did not report annual enrollment for FFY2000, the number shown is the number of children ever enrolled during the fourth quarter of FFY2000. This is a low estimate of the number of children ever enrolled during the year.

[g] Maine expanded coverage to 200% of the FPL on October 1,1999. The enrollment counts for FFY 2000 reflect this expansion. Approval of the state plan amendment to raise the income standard is pending.

[h] Maryland received approval on November 7, 2000, for a state plan amendment to implement a separate child health program on July 1, 2001.

[i] Maryland will raise its income eligibility standard to 300% of the FPL with the implementation of its separate child health program.

[j] Because the state did not report annual enrollment for FFY2000, the number shown is the number of children ever enrolled during the third quarter of FFY2000 (the most recent quarter for which the state provided data). This is a low estimate of the number of children ever enrolled during the year.

[k] New York has a net income standard of 192% of the FPL and a gross income standard of 230% of the FPL.

[l] Tennessee has a Medicaid section 1115 demonstration that has no upper income eligibility standards. TennCare enrollees with income above the poverty level are charged monthly premiums; the state subsidizes premiums for recipients with incomes up to 400% of the FPL. SCHIP covers only children born before October 1, 1983, in the expansion group who enrolled in TennCare on or after April 1, 1997.

[m] West Virginia folded its Medicaid expansion into its separate child health program, so that effective October 1, 2000, it has a separate child health program and is no longer a combination program.

[n] West Virginia raised its SCHIP income eligibility standard to 200% of the FPL effective November 1, 2000.

Table 2. SCHIP Program Allotments and Expenditures (In $1,000,000$) by State, FY1998 through FY2001

States	Available allotment amounts for FY1998-FY2001	Total expenditures applied against allotments (through 9/30/01)	% of available allotments spent (through 9/30/01)	Active allotment balance (through 9/30/01)				Total allotment balance
				FY1998	FY1999	FY2000	FY2001	
Alabama	307,716	98,959	32.2	—	x			208,756
Alaska*	45,469	45,469	100.0	—	—	—	—	-
Arizona	459,954	86,230	18.7	<				373,725
Arkansas	187,114	4,670	2.5	<				182,444
California	2,964,068	568,469	19.2	<				2,395,600
Colorado	168,602	44,886	26.6	—	x			123,716
Connecticut	144,871	38,242	26.4	—	x			106,629
Delaware	33,570	4,580	13.6	<				28,990
District of Columbia	44,605	11,539	25.9	—	x			33,066
Florida	970,544	378,265	39.0	—	x			592,278
Georgia	491,912	133,255	27.1—	x				43,355
Hawaii	36,535	3,463	9.5	<				424,756
Idaho	69,118	25,763	37.3	—	x			43,355
Illinois	517,341	92,584	17.9	<				424,756
Indiana[#]	308,786	175,383	56.8	—*	—			133,403
Iowa	127,920	51,179	40.0	—	x			76,742
Kansas	117,606	46,171	39.3	—	x			71,435
Kentucky[#]	239,515	145,994	61.0	—	—	x		93,521

States	Available allotment amounts for FY1998-FY2001	Total expenditures applied against allotments (through 9/30/01)	% of available allotments spent (through 9/30/01)	Active allotment balance (through 9/30/01)				Total allotment balance
				FY1998	FY1999	FY2000	FY2001	
Pennsylvania*	497,763	213,700	42.9	—**	x			284,063
Rhode Island*	42,177	31,015	73.5	—	—	x		11,161
South Carolina*	15,234	164,588	52.2	—**	—	x		150,647
South Dakota	31,794	9,885	31.1	—	x			21,909
Tennessee	283,858	56,145	19.8	<				227,713
Texas	1,905,329	345,279	18.1	<				1,560,050
Utah	104,546	43,394	41.5	—	x			61,151
Vermont	15,073	4,295	28.5	—	x			10,779
Virginia	269,524	52,477	19.5	—	x			217,048
Washington	190,015	6,139	3.2	<				183,876
West Virginia	84,847	32,968	38.9	—	x			51,879
Wisconsin	170,182	79,055	46.5	—	—	x		91,127
Wyoming	27,287	4,001	14.7	<				23,285
Total - 50 States and District of Columbia	16,815,848	5,516,828	32.8	NOT APPLICABLE				11,299,021
MOE	10,110	-	0.0	NOT APPLICABLE				10,110
Total Five Territories*	164,552	123,163	74.8					41,389
Total National	16,980,400	5,639,990	33.2					11,340,410

Source: Centers for Medicare and Medicaid Services, unpublished report (FY01RPT.xls, last updated December 12, 2001).

MOE refers to one of the maintenance of effort provisions in SCHIP statute. When SCHIP was created, three states-Florida, New York and Pennsylvania-had existing comprehensive state-based health benefit programs for children that were deemed to meet SCHIP requirements. These states are required to maintain their prior level of spending under SCHIP. Specifically, beginning in FY1999, the allotment for a given fiscal year will be reduced by the difference between the state's spending in the prior fiscal year versus fiscal year 1996 (before SCHIP began). The $10.1 million shown for MOE in this table reflects spending patterns in Pennsylvania for FY1998 and FY1999. In both years, Pennsylvania's share of SCHIP costs was less than FY1996 spending. Thus, Pennsylvania's SCHIP allotment for FY1999 and FY2000 has been reduced by $10.1 million combined, $2.2 million for FY1999 and $7.9 million for FY2000. These amounts will be included in the redistribution process for FY1999 and FY2000.

# indicates the 12 states that fully expended their original FY1998 allotments by the end of FY2000 as required, and therefore received additional "redistributed" FY1998 funds (see text for explanation). All five territories (Puerto Rico, Guam, Virgin Islands, American Samoa, and Northern Mariana Islands) also received redistributed FY1998 funds. The remaining 39 states (including the District of Columbia) did not spend their full FY1998 allotments by the end of FY2000. Such states received a "retained allotment" amount in the FY1998 redistribution process. Fourteen of these 39 states were still accessing their FY1998 retained allotments through 9/30/01 as indicated by the ^ in the FY1998 column above.

For the Active Allotment Account columns:

Blank means the fiscal year account had not yet been accessed. x designates the active account.
- means the fiscal year account had been fully expended.
^ means the state was applying expenditures against its FY1998 **retained** allotment
* means the state was applying expenditures against its FY1998 **redistributed** funds.
** means the state had not yet accessed its FY1998 **redistributed** funds.

Jurisdictions that exceeded available allotments and their excess expenditures through 9/30/01 (not shown above) were: (1) Alaska - $2,104, (2) American Samoa - $1.4 million, and (3) Northern Mariana Islands - $2.7 million.

Chapter 5

THE STATE CHILDREN'S HEALTH INSURANCE PROGRAM: ELIGIBILITY, ENROLLMENT, AND PROGRAM FUNDING[‡]

Evelyne P. Baumrucker

BACKGROUND

The Balanced Budget Act of 1997 (BBA 97, P.L. 105-33) established the State Children's Health Insurance Program (SCHIP) under a new Title XXI of the Social Security Act. Proposed regulations for the program were published on November 8, 1999 (*Federal Register*, v. 64, no. 215). The proposed regulation specifies rules governing the program.[1] Several recent laws have made technical and funding changes to Title XXI.[2]

[‡] Excerpted from CRS Report RL30642.

[1] An earlier proposed rule for the SCHIP program reported the allotments and grants to the states for FY1998 and FY1999 and appears in the Federal Register, v. 64, no. 42 [Thursday, March 4, 1999] Proposed Rule. The final rule for the State Children's Health Insurance Program's allotments and payments to states appeared in the *Federal Register*, v. 65, no. 101 [Wednesday, May 24, 2000] Rules and Regulations. This final rule provides final SCHIP program allotments for FY1998 through FY2000.

[2] For more details, see CRS Report RL30473, *State Children's Health Insurance Program: A Brief Overview,* by Elicia Herz and Evelyne Baumrucker. (Hereafter cited as RL30473, *State Children's Health Insurance Program*)

SCHIP is a federal-state partnership intended to provide health insurance coverage to low-income, uninsured children. SCHIP targets children in families whose annual incomes are higher than applicable Medicaid eligibility thresholds, and who do not have other health insurance coverage. In the original enacting statute Congress authorized and appropriated SCHIP federal matching grants in the amount of $39.7 billion for FY1998 through FY2007. Later, Congress provided additional appropriations for SCHIP in order to increase allocations to the territories, bringing the total of appropriations available for the period to almost $40 billion.

States may choose from three options when designing their SCHIP programs. They may expand their current Medicaid program, create a new, separate state insurance program, or devise a combination of both approaches. Under limited circumstances, states have the option to purchase a health benefits plan that is provided by a community-based health delivery system or to purchase family coverage under a group health plan as long as it is cost effective to do so.[3] As of late 1999, HCFA approved SCHIP plans for all 50 states, the District of Columbia and the five territories. As of July 3, 2000, 23 jurisdictions use Medicaid expansions (ME) and another 15 use separate state programs (SSP) for their SCHIP programs, with the remaining 18 providing health insurance coverage through a combination approach (COMBO).

ELIGIBILITY

The federal Medicaid statute mandates that states cover certain groups of children based on age and income criteria and gives states several options to expand coverage beyond these federal minimum standards. Children (and families) who meet the financial and categorical rules under the states' former Aid to Families with Dependent Children (AFDC) programs (in effect on July 16, 1996) are eligible for Medicaid even if they do not qualify for cash grants under the new Temporary Assistance for Needy Families (TANF) program. In addition, states *must* provide coverage to all pregnant

---

[3] In the case of community-based health delivery systems, the cost of coverage cannot exceed, on an average per child basis, the cost of coverage that would otherwise be provided. In the case of family coverage, the alternative must be cost-effective relative to the amount paid to obtain comparable coverage only of the targeted low-income children, and it must not substitute for health insurance coverage that would otherwise be provided to the children.

women and children age 5 and under living in families with incomes at or below 133% of the federal poverty level. States also *must* phase in coverage to children living in families with incomes below 100% of the federal poverty level who were born after September 30, 1983, until all such children under age 19 are covered.[4] As a result of this requirement, in FY2000 states must cover all children ages 6 to 16 whose family income is below the federal poverty threshold.[5]

States that wish to cover more children at higher levels of income, have the *option* of (1) making pregnant women and infants under 1 year of age up to 185% of the federal poverty level eligible for Medicaid; (2) using more liberal income and asset standards to determine eligibility than those required under law (as allowed under §1902(r)(2) of Medicaid law); and (3) using research and demonstration waivers (authorized under §1115 of the Social Security Act) to cover children who would not otherwise be eligible for the program. Forty-one states have expanded Medicaid eligibility for at least some children beyond federal mandates.[6] **Table 1** shows income limits for Medicaid eligibility as a percentage of the federal poverty level by age group in each of the 50 states and the District of Columbia, in effect on March 31, 1997.[7]

Under SCHIP, states may cover uninsured children in families with incomes that are above the state's applicable Medicaid eligibility standard but less than 200% of the federal poverty level. However, states, in which the maximum Medicaid income level for children was at or above 200% federal poverty level as of March 31, 1997,[8] may increase this income level

---

[4] Medicaid eligibility for all low-income children born after September 30, 1983 was mandated in the Omnibus Budget Reconciliation Act of 1990 (OBRA-90).

[5] These children are commonly referred to as the "Waxman Kids" after Representative Henry Waxman of California who spearheaded eligibility expansions for children and pregnant women under Medicaid in the late 1980s.

[6] As of October 1997, 35 states used various options available to them to exceed the federal minimum mandate of 133% federal poverty level for pregnant women and infants. Thirteen states expanded eligibility for children ages 1 through 5 above this same mandatory minimum (133% FPL). Twenty-eight states moved beyond the federal mandate of 100% FPL and/or age requirements for children ages 6 and older. See Henneberry, Joan. *State Medicaid Coverage of Pregnant Women and Children*. NGA Center for Best Practices, Health Policy Studies Division, September 30, 1997.

[7] The proposed rule for the SCHIP program (published in the *Federal Register*, v. 64, no. 215, November 8, 1999) suggests a change to the official start date of SCHIP. If approved, the date to which income eligibility is keyed will change from March 31, 1997 to June 1, 1997. While few states will be affected by the change, the new start date will represent the lower bounds for income eligibility in the SCHIP program.

[8] Ibid.

by an additional 50 percentage points under SCHIP, even if the resulting income limit exceeds 200% of the federal poverty level.

Not all targeted low-income uninsured children will necessarily receive medical assistance under SCHIP for two reasons. First, unlike Medicaid, federal law does not establish an *individual* entitlement to benefits under SCHIP. Instead, it entitles *states* with approved SCHIP plans to pre-determined federal allotments based on a distribution formula set in the law. Second, states are allowed under the law to define the group of targeted low-income children who may enroll in SCHIP. Title XXI allows states to use the following characteristics in determining eligibility: geography, age, income and resources, residency, disability status, access to other health insurance, and duration of eligibility for SCHIP coverage.

In addition to the Medicaid eligibility thresholds in effect at the start of the SCHIP program, **Table 1** shows how the states, the District of Columbia, and the territories[9] will use SCHIP funds to expand eligibility thresholds beyond those applicable under Medicaid. The table shows the type of SCHIP program implemented as well as the targeted age groups affected. A majority of the states are expanding eligibility to levels between 150% and 200% FPL. In one state, New Jersey, the upper income eligibility limit for Medicaid expansions and separate state programs under SCHIP has reached 350% of the federal poverty level.

While expansions in coverage have been achieved for all age groups of children under SCHIP, the most significant increases in eligibility benefit older adolescents. States are taking advantage of the opportunity to use enhanced matching funds under SCHIP to cover a portion of the older teens ages 16-18 in families with incomes up to 100% of the federal poverty level sooner than required under current Medicaid law. In many cases, states are also expanding their programs to cover children of all ages in families with income well above the 100% FPL requirement.

At the start of the SCHIP program many states submitted Medicaid expansions as place-holder plans to ensure their access to the enhanced matching funding available through SCHIP. These early Medicaid expansions were used to create more uniformity in income eligibility criteria (e.g., provide coverage to at least 100% FPL) for all children under the age of 18. As the program has evolved, states have submitted amendments to their original Medicaid expansions to define separate state programs that

---

[9] The five territories are American Samoa, the Commonwealth of the Northern Mariana Islands, Guam, Puerto Rico, and the Virgin Islands.

further expand eligibility thresholds. Of the 29 state plan amendments that expand eligibility in some way, 10 build on their original submission to create combination programs in the states. Fourteen eligibility-related amendments increased thresholds beyond the limits defined in the state's original submission. Five amendments have had the effect of expanding eligibility under SCHIP by modifying methods of counting income through the use of income disregards.[10]

ENROLLMENT

The SCHIP program is nearing its third year of existence. While significant headway has been made by the states in the development and implementation of their SCHIP programs, given complications associated with starting a new program, enrollment numbers have not kept pace with expectations. Early enrollment estimates from HCFA[11] indicated that nearly 1 million children (982,000) were enrolled in SCHIP under 43 operational state programs as of December 1998. More recently, HCFA reported that nearly 2 million children (1,979,450) were enrolled in SCHIP during FY1999 under 53 operational state programs.[12] Over 1.2 million of these children were served by separate programs and almost 700,000 were enrolled in Medicaid expansions. Subsequent to the enactment of BBA 97, CBO estimated that SCHIP would cover an average of 2.3 million children per year after 1999.[13] The Administration's goal is to enroll 5 million children in SCHIP by FY2002.[14]

---

[10] For determining income eligibility for SCHIP and Medicaid, some states may apply "income disregards." These are specified dollar amounts subtracted from gross income to compute net income, which is then compared to the applicable income criterion. Such disregards increase the effective income level above the stated standard. SCHIP state plans do not consistently report the use of income disregards, nor whether the stated income standards include or exclude such disregards.

[11] Health Care Financing Administration. *A Preliminary Estimate of the Children's Health Insurance Program Aggregate Enrollment Numbers Through December 31, 1998* (background only). April 20, 1999.

[12] Health Care Financing Administration. *The State Children's Health Insurance Program. Annual Enrollment Report, October 1, 1998-September 30, 1999.* (no date)

[13] U.S. Congressional Budget Office. *Expanding Health Insurance Coverage for Children Under Title XXI of the Social Security Act* (CBO Memorandum). February 1998.

[14] For more detail on the state by state enrollment patterns in SCHIP, see CRS Report RL30556, *Reaching Low-Income, Uninsured Children: Are Medicaid and SCHIP Doing the Job?* by Elicia Herz, Evelyne Baumrucker, and Jennifer Gillespie and CRS Report RL30473, *State Children's Health Insurance Program: A Brief Overview*, by Elicia Herz and Evelyne Baumrucker.

PROGRAM FUNDING

Appropriations for FY1998 through FY2000

The original enacting statute provided appropriations for SCHIP for FY1998 through FY2007. The statute authorizes and appropriates these funds in advance of any appropriations act so that the SCHIP program operates like a mandatory spending program. The appropriation committees do, however, have the authority to increase, defer, or rescind funding for the SCHIP program and on several occasions have considered proposals to do so. On three occasions, Congress has increased appropriations for SCHIP, and on two occasions considered proposals to reduce funding for the program.[15]

The law[16] sets forth methodologies and procedures to determine state-specific allotments of federal funds for each federal fiscal year; these are described below. DHHS issues final rules in the *Federal Register* that enumerate specific state allotments. A total of $4.295 billion in federal matching funds was available to the states and territories for FY1998.[17] Of this total appropriation, the amount available for allotment to the 50 states and the District of Columbia was $4.224 billion. An additional $10.738 million was set-aside for allotment to the territories, as was another $60 million for Special Diabetes Grants.[18]

For FY1999, $4.307 billion in federal matching funds was appropriated for the states and territories. For this year, an additional $32 million was appropriated for allotment to the territories under the FY1999 Omnibus Appropriations Act, (P.L. 105-277). These new funds brought the FY1999 federal funds available to the territories for SCHIP to $42.690 million. The states and the District of Columbia will share $4.204 billion, and $60 million is available for diabetes grants for FY1999.

---

[15] For more information see CRS Report RS20628, *State Children's Health Insurance Program (SCHIP): FY2000 and FY2001 Appropriations,* by Evelyne Baumrucker.

[16] *Federal Register,* v. 65, no. 101, May 24, 2000.

[17] P.L. 105-100, §162(8)(a), struck out "$4,275,000,000" and substituted "$4,295,000,000," effective as if included in the enactment of P.L. 105-33, August 5, 1997.

[18] The original authorizing legislation for SCHIP requires that .25% of the program's total authorization be set-aside for the territories. In addition, the law requires that the amount available to the 50 states and the District of Columbia be further reduced (after the set-aside to the territories) by $60,000,000; $30,000,000 each for a special diabetes research program for Type I diabetes and for special diabetes programs for Native Americans. The diabetes programs are funded for FY1998 through FY2002 only.

For FY2000, SCHIP appropriations total $4.309 billion. The amount of federal funds available for distribution to the states and the District of Columbia is $4.204 billion. The territories will receive $44.890 million, consisting of their original FY2000 allotment plus an additional sum of $34.200 million provided by P.L. 106-113, the Balanced Budget Refinement Act. Again, $60 million is set aside for diabetes grants.[19]

Allotments among the States

For each fiscal year, the states and the District of Columbia are allotted a "proportion" of the total amount of title XXI dollars available for that year. A state's proportion refers to the amount of the allotment for a state for a given fiscal year divided by the total amount available nationally for all states for that fiscal year. The state proportions are determined by a two-step process described below.

Under the first step, each state's proportion is calculated as the product of two components: the Number of Children Factor and the State Cost Factor. In general, the Number of Children Factor is the combination of the number of low-income children regardless of insurance status, and the number of low-income, uninsured children residing in a state for a given fiscal year.[20] The State Cost Factor is the sum of .85 multiplied by the ratio of the annual average wages per employee in the health services industry for the year to the national average wages per such employee for the year, and .15. For each fiscal year and state, counts of children are 3-year averages taken from recent March Supplements of the Current Population Survey. Employee wages are 3-year averages as reported by the Bureau of Labor Statistics.

The definition of the Number of Children Factor in this formula varies across fiscal years. For FY1998 and FY1999 only, this factor is defined as

---

[19] The Balanced Budget Refinement Act provided additional funding for SCHIP-related issues. For each of the FY2000 through FY2007, $10 million is provided to the Secretary of Commerce to make appropriate adjustments to the annual Current Population Survey (CPS) to improve the reliability of state-specific estimates of the number of low-income uninsured children. In addition, for FY2000, $10 million is provided for a new federal evaluation of the SCHIP program. For more details on changes made to the Medicaid and SCHIP programs by P.L. 106-133, see CRS Repor t RL30400, *Medicaid and the State Children's Health Insurance Program (SCHIP): Provisions in the Consolidated Appropriations Act for FY2000* by Jean Hearne and Elicia Herz. (Hereafter cited as CRS Report RL30400, *Medicaid and the State Children's Health Insurance Program*)

[20] Low-income is defined as a family with income below 200% of the federal poverty level.

the 3-year average of uninsured children in families with income below 200% FPL. For FY2000 only, for each state this factor is the sum of 75% of the number of low-income uninsured children, and 25% of the number of low-income children. For FY2001 through FY2007, for each state this factor is the sum of 50% of the number of low-income, uninsured children and 50% of the number of low-income children.

In the second step, floors, ceilings, and a reconciliation process are applied to the "preadjusted" proportions determined in step one. The SCHIP statute specifies three minimum proportions that must be applied when determining each state's allotment: (1) the program floor for every state is $2 million; (2) for each fiscal year, the floor will not be less than 90% of a state's allotment proportion for the preceding year; and (3) the floor is set at 70% of the proportion for FY1999. The state's proportion must not go below any of these three floors. Comparably, each state's proportion for a fiscal year is also limited by a maximum ceiling. The ceiling is equal to 145% of a state's allotment proportion for FY1999. Finally, the sum of the "preadjusted" proportions for all states must be equal to one. If they are not, the allotment proportions will be subject to a reconciliation process. Under the reconciliation process, if the application of the floors and ceilings across states results in a surplus for a given year, HCFA must apply a pro-rata increase for all states below the ceiling. If the distribution creates a deficit in a given year, there will be a ceiling in the maximum increase permitted in that year to ensure budget neutrality.

A state's final annual allotment is then calculated by multiplying the state's "adjusted" proportion for that fiscal year by the national total appropriated in that year. Final allotments are published in the *Federal Register*.

Payments to the States

To receive federal funds, states must submit a plan describing their program to the Health Care Financing Administration (HCFA) for approval. In order to access FY1998 allotments, states must have received such approval prior to October 1, 1999. All states had approved plans by the deadline. Funds not drawn down from a state's federal allotment by the end of each fiscal year will continue to be available for 2 additional fiscal years, giving each state a total of 3 years to spend its allotment of federal matching funds from a given fiscal year. A state must draw down its entire allotment from a given fiscal year before it may access the next year's funding. FY1998 money not spent by the end of FY2000 (as of September 30, 2000) will be redistributed by a method, to be determined by the Secretary of HHS, to states that have fully expended their existing FY1998 allotments, and are able to provide matching funds. These states will have 1 year to spend the redistributed funds. Redistributed funds not spent by the end of the fiscal year in which they are reallotted will officially expire.

Federal law limits the funds available to pay for the administrative costs of SCHIP to 10% of spending for benefits in any given year. Activities included in the 10% cap consist of (1) costs incurred through data collection, assessment of the state plan, quality assurance activities, eligibility determination, performance measurements, outreach and coordination initiatives, and public involvement, (2) health benefit coverage of specialty and sub-speciality care, and (3) special initiatives for improving the health of children.

Many states are concerned that the 10% administrative cap will limit their ability to fund outreach initiatives necessary to find and enroll eligible children. Because the 10% cap is applied to the total benefit payments made to a state in any year (10% of the money a state actually draws down, as opposed to its full allotment), states have questioned whether there will be sufficient funds available to pay the substantial start-up costs of their SCHIP programs. In response to these concerns, HCFA has published guidance that gives states some flexibility on the 10% cap.

States that chose Medicaid expansions can claim federal matching funds for administrative and outreach expenditures either through the regular Medicaid program at the applicable Medicaid federal matching rate or under SCHIP at the enhanced matching rate. This allows states to spread out their administrative costs across two programs. States also have the option to delay the submission of claims for administrative expenditures to HCFA for up to 2 years from the date of the expenditure. This process allows states with low benefit expenditures in the early years of their program to maximize reimbursement for administrative expenditures at the enhanced federal matching rate.

Tables 2, 3, and 4 provide SCHIP program funding information for the states and territories for FY1998, FY1999 and FY2000 respectively. The second column of each table shows total allotments of federal funds. Allotment amounts for FY2001 (and beyond) will be published in the *Federal Register*.

Like Medicaid, SCHIP is a federal-state matching program. For each dollar of state spending, the federal government will make a matching payment. The third and fourth columns of **Tables 2, 3, and 4** provide Federal Medical Assistance Percentages (FMAP)[21] and Enhanced Federal Medical Assistance Percentages (Enhanced FMAP). Under Medicaid, a state's share of program spending is equal to 100% minus the FMAP for the state. Under SCHIP, the Enhanced FMAP is equal to the state's Medicaid FMAP increased by the number of percentage points that is equal to 30% multiplied by the number of percentage points by which the FMAP is less than 100%. For example, if a state has a Medicaid FMAP of 50%, under Medicaid the state must spend 50 cents for every 50 cents that the federal government contributes. The Enhanced FMAP would be equal to the Medicaid federal matching percentage increased by 15 percentage points, (50% + (30% multiplied by 50%) = 65%). The state share under SCHIP would be equal to 100% - 65% = 35%.

Compared with Medicaid FMAPs, which ranged from 50% to 76.8% in FY2000, the Enhanced FMAP for the SCHIP programs ranged from 65% to 83.76%. The Enhanced FMAP applies to all SCHIP assistance for targeted low-income children, including child health coverage provided through a Medicaid expansion. The FMAP and Enhanced FMAP are subject to ceilings of 83% and 85%, respectively.

The totals in the fifth, sixth, and final columns of **Tables 2, 3, and 4** are estimates of the required state match necessary to claim the maximum federal SCHIP allotments; estimates of the ratio of federal dollars spent to each state dollar; and estimates of potential total program expenditures (state share + federal share), respectively. Because states have 3 years to draw down a given year's funding and the Enhanced FMAPs are variable from year to year, it is not possible to report a precise dollar amount in these columns. The Enhanced FMAP used to determine the required state match is based on the date the state makes a payment to cover a SCHIP claim.[22] The state then submits claims for these payments to HCFA on a quarterly expenditure report. Once state claims have been approved by HCFA, the federal portion is paid to the state using the oldest open allotment and the Enhanced FMAP applicable to the date the state made specific payments to providers. For example, assume a state makes a payment to a provider in

---

[21] FMAP is a measure of the 3-year average per capita income in each state squared, compared to that of the nation as a whole.

[22] *Federal Register*, v. 65, no. 101, May 24, 2000 and Federal Register, 45 CFR Parts 92 and 95, May 24, 2000.

April of FY2000. If the state then submits its corresponding claim to HCFA on its FY2000, third quarter expenditure report and the state's FY1998 allotted funds are still available, then the federal dollars paid to the state for that claim will be paid out of the FY1998 allotment and the amount will be based on the state's FY2000 Enhanced FMAP.

Spending

Spending projections in the first 2 years of the program are consistent with HCFA's enrollment figures and fall well below total federal appropriation levels. Federal spending in FY1998 totaled less than $500 million. CBO estimates that federal SCHIP spending will total approximately $1 billion for FY1999 and $2 billion for FY2000.[23] For each of these years, total annual federal appropriation levels are approximately $4.3 billion. Based on actual spending and projections through February 2000, HCFA estimates that about $1.9 billion may remain unspent from the FY1998 allotments by the end of FY2000 and will be subject to redistribution in early FY2001.[24] At that point in time, only 12 states and three territories were expected to claim their full FY1998 allotments. It is to early to determine whether states will ultimately claim their full FY1999 and FY2000 federal SCHIP funding.[25]

---

[23] U.S. Congressional Budget Office. *The Budget and Economic Outlook: Fiscal Years 2001-2010*. Washington, GPO, March 2000.
[24] HCFA's FY1998 SCHIP spending projections are based on state submitted actual expenditures through FY1999 and state submitted expenditure estimates for FY2000 through February of this year (HCFA, unpublished data, April 4, 2000).
[25] For more information on SCHIP in the FY2000 and FY2001 appropriations process, see CRS Report RS20628, *State Children's Health Insurance Program (SCHIP): FY2000 and FY2001 Appropriations*, by Evelyne P. Baumrucker.

Table 1. Medicaid and SCHIP Income and Age Related Eligibility Criteria as a Percent of the Federal Poverty Level

	Medicaid Standards in Effect 3/31/97 (lower income boundary for SCHIP)[a,b]				SCHIP (In Effect 7/7/00)[c]									
					Medicaid expansion					Separate state plan				
States	Age 0 to 1[e]	Ages 1 thru 5[e]	Ages 6 thru 14[e]	Ages 15 thru 18[f]	All ages 0-18	Preg. teens and infants[d]	Children below age 6[e]	Children age 6 and over (Through upper age limit)	Children 16-18	All ages 0-18	Preg. teens and infants[d]	Children below age 6[e]	Children ages 6 and over (Through upper age limit)	Children 16-18
Alabama	133	133	100	15	–	–	–	–	100	200	–	–	–	–
Alaska	133	133	100	100	200	–	–	–	–	–	–	–	–	–
American Samoa[g]	–	–	–	–	–	–	–	–	–	–	–	–	–	–
Arizona	140	133	100	30	–	–	–	–	–	200	–	–	–	–
Arkansas[h]	133	133	100	18	–	–	–	–	100 (born after 9/30/82 and before 10/1/83)	–	–	–	–	–
California	200	133	100	82	–	–	–	–	100	250	–	–	–	–
Colorado	133	133	100	37	–	–	–	–	–	185 (0-17)	–	–	–	–
Connecticut	185	185	185	100	–	–	–	–	185	300[i]	–	–	–	–

	Medicaid Standards in Effect 3/31/97 (lower income boundary for SCHIP)[a,b]				SCHIP (In Effect 7/7/00)[c]									
					Medicaid expansion					Separate state plan				
States	Age 0 to 1[d]	Ages 1 thru 5[e]	Ages 6 thru 14[f]	Ages 15 thru 18[g]	All ages 0-18	Preg. teens and infants[h]	Children below age 6[i]	Children age 6 and over (Through upper age limit)	Children 16-18	All ages 0-18	Preg. teens and infants[h]	Children below age 6[i]	Children ages 6 and over (Through upper age limit)	Children 16-18
Delaware	133	133	100	100	–	–	–	–	–	200	–	–	–	–
District of Columbia	185	133	100	50	200	–	–	–	–	–	–	–	–	–
Florida[j]	185	133	100	28	–	–	–	–	100	200	–	–	–	–
Georgia	185	133	100	100	–	–	–	–	–	200	–	–	–	–
Guam[k]	–	–	–	–	–	–	–	–	–	–	–	–	–	–
Hawaii[j]	185	133	100	100	–	–	185 (1-6)	–	–	–	–	–	–	–
Idaho	133	133	100	100	150	–	–	–	–	–	–	–	–	–
Illinois	133	133	100	46	–	200	–	133 (6-18)	–	185 (1-18)	–	–	–	–
Indiana	150	133	100	100	150 (1-18)	–	–	–	–	200	–	–	–	–
Iowa	185	133	100	37	–	–	–	–	133 (6-18)	185 (1-18)	–	–	–	–
Kansas	150	133	100	100	–	–	–	–	–	200 (0-18)	–	–	–	–

	Medicaid Standards in Effect 3/31/97 (lower income boundary for SCHIP)**				SCHIP (In Effect 7/7/00)									
					Medicaid expansion					Separate state plan				
States	Age 0 to 1*	Ages 1 thru 5*	Ages 6 thru 14*	Ages 15 thru 18*	All ages 0-18	Preg. teens and infants*	Children below age 6*	Children age 6 and over (Through upper age limit)	Children 16-18	All ages 0-18	Preg. teens and infants*	Children below age 6*	Children age 6 and over (Through upper age limit)	Children 16-18
Kentucky	185	133	100	33	150 (1-18)	–	–	–	–	200	–	–	–	–
Louisiana	133	133	100	10	150	–	–	–	–	–	–	–	–	–
Maine	185	133	125	125	150 (1-18)	–	–	–	–	185 (1-18)	–	–	–	–
Maryland	185	185	185	100	200*	–	–	–	–	–	–	–	–	–
Massachusetts	185	133	114	86	150 (1-18)	–	–	–	–	200	–	–	–	–
Michigan	185	133	100	100	–	–	–	–	150	200	–	–	–	–
Minnesota	275	275	275	275	–	280 (0-2)	–	–	–	–	–	–	–	–
Mississippi	185	133	100	34	–	–	–	–	100	200	–	–	–	–
Missouri*	185	133	100	100	200	–	–	–	–	–	–	–	–	–
Montana	133	133	100	40.5	–	–	–	–	–	150	–	–	–	–
Nebraska	150	133	100	33	185	–	–	–	–	–	–	–	–	–
Nevada	133	133	100	31	–	–	–	–	–	200	–	–	–	–

	Medicaid Standards in Effect 3/31/97 (lower income boundary for SCHIP)^a					SCHIP (In Effect 7/7/00)^c								
						Medicaid expansion					Separate state plan			
States	Age 0 to 1^d	Ages 1 thru 5^e	Ages 6 thru 14^f	Ages 15 thru 18^g	All ages 0-18	Preg. teens and infants^h	Children below age 6^i	Children age 6 and over (Through upper age limit)	Children 16-18	All ages 0-18	Preg. teens and infants^h	Children below age 6^i	Children ages 6 and over (Through upper age limit)	Children 16-18
New Hampshire	185	185	185	185		300 (0-1 only)	–	–	–	300 (1-18)^y	–	–	–	–
New Jersey	185	133	100	41	–	–	–	133 (6-18)	–	350	–	–	–	–
New Mexico	185	185	185	185	235	–	–	–	–	–	–	–	–	–
New York^z	185	133	100	51	–	–	–	–	100	192	–	–	–	–
North Carolina	185	133	100	100	–	–	–	–	–	200	–	–	–	–
Northern Marianas^t	–	–	–	–	–	–	–	–	–	–	–	–	–	–
North Dakota	133	133	100	100 (thru age 17)	–	–	–	–	100 (18 only)	140	–	–	–	–
Ohio	133	133	100	33	200	–	–	–	–	–	–	–	–	–
Oklahoma	150	133	100	48	185 (0-17 and preg. teens)	–	–	–	–	–	–	–	–	–
Oregon	133	133	100	100	–	–	–	–	–	170	–	–	–	–
Pennsylvania^j	185	133	100	41	–	–	–	–	–	200^r	–	–	–	–

	Medicaid Standards in Effect 3/31/97 (lower income boundary for SCHIP)ᵃᵃ					SCHIP (In Effect 7/7/00)ʸ								
						Medicaid expansion					Separate state plan			
States	Age 0 to 1ᵃ	Ages 1 thru 5ᶜ	Ages 6 thru 14ᵈ	Ages 15 thru 18ᶠ	All ages 0-18	Preg-teens and infantsᵈ	Children below age 6ᶜ	Children age 6 and over (Through upper age limit)	Children 16-18	All ages 0-18	Preg-teens and infantsᵈ	Children below age 6ᶜ	Children age 6 and over (Through upper age limit)	Children 16-18
Puerto Ricoⁱ	–	–	–	–	200 (0-18)ʸ	–	–	–	–	–	–	–	–	–
Rhode Island	250	250 (thru age 7)	100 (ages 8 thru 14)	100	–	–	–	250 (8-18)ʸ	–	–	–	–	–	–
South Carolina	185	*	*	*	150 (1-18)*	–	–	–	–	–	–	–	–	–
South Dakota	133	133	100	100	140	–	–	–	–	–	–	–	–	–
Tennesseeᵉ	–	–	–	16	–	–	–	–	100 (17-18)ʸ	–	–	–	–	–
Texas	185	133	100	17	–	–	–	–	100	200	–	–	–	–
Utah	133	133	100	100 (thru age 17)	–	–	–	–	–	200	–	–	–	–
Vermont	225	225	225	225	–	–	–	–	–	300 (0-17)*	–	–	–	–
Virginia	133	133	100	100	–	–	–	–	–	185	–	–	–	–
Virgin Islandsᵉ	–	–	–	–	Family of four <$8,500 annually	–	–	–	–	–	–	–	–	–

	Medicaid Standards in Effect 3/31/97 (lower income boundary for SCHIP)[a,b]				SCHIP (In Effect 7/7/00)[c]							
					Medicaid expansion				Separate state plan			
States	Age 0 to 1[d]	Ages 1 thru 5[e]	Ages 6 thru 14[e]	Ages 15 thru 18[e]	All ages 0-18	Preg. teens and infants[a]	Children below age 6[e]	Children age 6 and over (Through upper age limit)	Children 16-18	All ages 0-18	Preg. teens and infants[a]	Children below age 6[e]	Children ages 6 and over (Through upper age limit)	Children 16-18
Washington	200	200	200	200	—	—	—	—	—	250	—	—	—	—
West Virginia	150	133	100	100	—	—	150 (1-5)	—	—	—	—	—	150	—
Wisconsin	185	185	100	45	—	—	185 (6-18y)	—	—	—	—	—	—	—
Wyoming	133	133	100	55	—	—	—	—	—	—	—	—	133	—

Source: CRS analysis of submitted state plans and amendments.

[a] Title XXI contains a provision that a child's family income must exceed the applicable Medicaid income level that was in effect on March 31, 1997 in order for that child to be eligible for SCHIP-funded coverage. If approved, the proposed rule (published in the *Federal Register*, vol. 64, no. 215, Monday November 8, 1999) will change that date from March 31, 1997 to June 1, 1997–a change that will affect income eligibility in a few states. These percentages represent the lower income boundary for the SCHIP program. Information for the Medicaid eligibility portion of this table comes from the Health Care Financing Administration, *The State Children's Health Insurance Program; Annual Enrollment Report; October 1, 1998 through September 30, 1999;* January 2000.

[b] In 34 states, children may also qualify for Medicaid through medically needy programs (data not shown). In most cases, income criteria for medically needy programs are above AFDC-related standards but less than 133% of the federal poverty level.

[c] The 2000 federal poverty guideline for a family of three is $14,150 per year; for Alaska $17,690; and for Hawaii $16,270.

[d] To be eligible as an infant, a child is under age 1 and has not yet reached his or her first birthday.

[e] To be eligible in this category, the child is age 1 or older, but has not yet reached his or her 6th birthday.

[f] Federal law requires states to provide Medicaid to children in families with incomes that meet the state's former Aid to Families with Dependent Children (AFDC) income eligibility standards in effect on July 16, 1996. In addition, since July 1, 1991, states (under OBRA 1990) have been required to cover all

children under age 19, who were born after September 30, 1983, and whose family income is below 100% of the federal poverty level. The 1983 start date means that the mandatory coverage is extended to children by one age cohort each year until reaching those under age 19 in FY2002. If a state has expanded eligibility to older children beyond the OBRA 1990 mandate, the former AFDC standard as it applies to Medicaid eligibility is not applicable. The data in this column reflect the federal minimum requirements of states for children ages 15 and older on March 31, 1997 (see footnote "a"). The eligibility levels recorded in this column were in effect at the start of the SCHIP program and thus represent the lower income boundary for SCHIP.

g In American Samoa, eligibility for Medicaid and SCHIP are determined based on a system of presumptive eligibility. American Samoa does not use a system of individual eligibility determinations. Each year the percentage of the population that falls below the American Samoan poverty level is estimated and, after approval of the estimate, HCFA pays a capitated amount for Medicaid based on that percentage.

h Arkansas increased Medicaid eligibility to 200% FPL effective September 1997 through a §1115 demonstration authority.

i State-sponsored health insurance will be available to all uninsured children in Connecticut. If the family's income is above 300% federal poverty level, the family will be expected to pay premiums and cost-sharing to access services. For children with family incomes greater than 300% federal poverty level, only state dollars will be used for funding.

j These states had state-funded programs that existed prior to SCHIP. Title XXI permitted children in these state-funded programs to be covered under SCHIP and required these states to maintain their previous levels of state spending.

k In Guam, Medicaid and SCHIP eligibility determinations are made by the Department of Public Health and Social Services. The Medicaid program claims federal financial participation (FFP) only for covered services to the categorically needy.

l Hawaii's coverage of pregnant women and children is through Hawaii QUEST, a §1115 waiver managed care program.

m On January 3, 2000, the state submitted an amendment to its approved Title XXI plan which allows for a 20% deduction to earned income in determining eligibility for the Hawk-I program and includes an additional managed health care plan, Unity Choice, from Wellmark Health Plan of Iowa.

n Maryland submitted an amendment January 3, 2000 that amends its §1115 demonstration waiver to implement state legislation enacted in the 1999 legislative session. It imposes a premium on children whose families have incomes above 185% FPL enrolled in the Maryland Children's Health Program by July 1, 2000.

o Missouri will use Title XXI funds to expand its Medicaid program to children up to age 18 with family incomes up to 200% federal poverty level; Missouri will cover children with family incomes between 200-300% of the federal poverty level at its regular Medicaid FMAP through an §1115 Medicaid Waiver. The §1115 waiver allows the state to charge cost sharing payments to eligible families between 185-300% of the federal poverty level for children between the ages 0-18.

p New Hampshire will apply an income disregard to determine eligibility for SCHIP.

q The Northern Mariana Islands do not have an AFDC or TANF program. However, it is the only U.S. Territory that does have Supplemental Security Income (SSI), and its entire Medicaid program is based on SSI requirements. All individuals receiving SSI cash payments are eligible for Medicaid. All other individuals who meet the income and resource standards for SSI, with the standard exemptions and deductions, are also eligible. In addition, although the

Northern Mariana Islands do not have a medically needy program, anyone can spend down to become eligible for any month in which medical costs reduce income to the appropriate level.

r Pennsylvania uses state funds to extend coverage up to 235% of the federal poverty level for all children up to their 19th birthday.

s Puerto Rico's Medicaid program extends covered services to both the categorically needy (TANF) and the medically needy. There is no SSI, rather the former mainland classifications of Old Age Assistance, Aid to the Blind, Aid to the Permanently and Totally Disabled, exist. Although mandated on the mainland, the Commonwealth has not opted to cover poverty level groups, and is exempt from requirements linking the "medically needy" income levels to "categorically needy" (formerly AFDC) income levels. The medically needy income level for a family of four is $8,220 with a resource level of $900. The yearly categorically needy standard for a family of four is $1,536.

t Rhode Island expanded Medicaid eligibility up to 250% federal poverty level through a §1115 waiver. Benefits for children age 8 thru age 18 under this waiver will be financed by Title XXI funds and are considered the state's Medicaid Expansion under SCHIP. HCFA approved eligibility up to 300% FPL as submitted in the state's original plan submission, but the Rhode Island state legislature has not approved this expansion.

u In August of 1997, the South Carolina state legislature approved an expansion of the state's Medicaid program to cover all children in families with incomes less than 150% federal poverty level up to age 19. Because Title XXI was created just months later (October of 1997) HCFA approved the use of Title XXI funds for this expansion. Cells were left blank in the Medicaid columns to underscore that the expansion to Medicaid in the state is funded by Title XXI.

v TennCare offers health insurance for uninsured families at any income level. Premiums are charged on a sliding fee scale based on family size and income. Uninsured enrollees from families with incomes above 400% federal poverty level are charged a monthly premium based on a higher sliding fee scale than for those below 400% federal poverty level. Through SCHIP, the state will extend eligibility to uninsured children born before October 1, 1983, who are under age 19 in families with incomes at or below 100% of the federal poverty level and who could not have been enrolled under the operating rules for the state's Medicaid demonstration program before April 1, 1997. TennCare's eligibility for this population was officially closed on March 31, 1997 because they had exhausted state and federal dollars at the regular Medicaid FMAP. The state can cover this population with Title XXI enhanced matching funds since this group was not covered by Medicaid at the date specified in the SCHIP legislation, and therefore would be eligible for SCHIP.

w In Vermont Title XXI funds are used to cover children through their 17 birthday up to 300% FPL. Vermont also covers under-insured children through age 17 up to 300% FPL using a §1115 Medicaid waiver with §1902(r)(2) cost-sharing requirements.

x The Virgin Islands cover the medically needy, and persons in families with an annual income less than $8,500. There is an income disregard of $1,800 for specified resources. HCFA approved a state plan amendment on February 4, 2000 that permits the use of SCHIP monies to pay any medical expenses incurred after the Virgin Islands runs out of Medicaid federal dollars. Previously, SCHIP payments were restricted for payments to hospitals and clinics. The amendment allows the Virgin Islands to pay inpatient pediatric medical bills incurred by an approved medical provider for children less than age 19 in the territory's hospitals.

y Once a family is enrolled, eligibility is maintained until income exceeds 200% federal poverty level. Wisconsin may receive enhanced Title XXI FMAP to cover both parents and children if the cost-effectiveness of family coverage is demonstrated. Also, Wisconsin may cover families through employer-sponsored insurance when it is demonstrated to be cost-effective.

Table 2. Financial Program Information for States and Territories FY1998[a]

State (or other territory)	Total federal allotments in dollars FY1998[b]	FMAP % FY1998[c]	Enhanced FMAP % FY1998[c]	Estimated state match for maximum federal allocation in dollars FY1998[c]	Estimated federal dollars for each state dollar[d]	Estimated total program expenditures in dollars (federal share +state share FY1998)[d]
Alabama	85,975,213	69.32	78.52	23,519,455	3.66	109,494,668
Alaska	6,889,296	59.80	71.86	2,697,812	2.55	9,587,108
American Samoa	128,850	50.00	65.00	69,381	1.86	198,231
Arizona	116,797,799	65.33	75.73	37,431,435	3.12	154,229,234
Arkansas	47,907,958	72.84	80.99	11,244,972	4.26	59,152,930
California	854,644,807	51.23	65.86	443,024,198	1.93	1,297,669,005
Colorado	41,790,547	51.97	66.38	21,165,987	1.97	62,956,534
Connecticut	34,959,075	50.00	65.00	18,824,117	1.86	53,783,192
Delaware	8,053,463	50.00	65.00	4,336,480	1.86	12,389,943
District of Columbia	12,076,002	70.00	79.00	3,210,076	3.76	15,286,078
Florida	270,214,724	55.65	68.96	121,627,973	2.22	391,842,697
Georgia	124,660,136	60.84	72.59	47,071,695	2.65	171,731,831
Guam	375,813	50.00	65.00	202,361	1.86	578,174
Hawaii	8,945,304	50.00	65.00	4,816,702	1.86	13,762,006
Idaho	15,879,707	69.59	78.71	4,295,248	3.70	20,174,955
Illinois	122,528,573	50.00	65.00	65,976,924	1.86	188,505,497
Indiana	70,512,432	61.41	72.99	26,093,174	2.70	96,605,606

State (or other territory)	Total federal allotments in dollars FY1998[b]	FMAP % FY1998[c]	Enhanced FMAP % FY1998[c]	Estimated state match for maximum federal allocation in dollars FY1998[d]	Estimated federal dollars for each state dollar[d]	Estimated total program expenditures in dollars (federal share +state share FY1998)[d]
Iowa	32,460,463	63.75	74.63	11,034,731	2.94	43,495,194
Kansas	30,656,520	59.71	71.80	12,040,583	2.55	42,697,103
Kentucky	49,932,527	70.37	79.26	13,065,867	3.82	62,998,394
Louisiana	101,736,841	70.03	79.02	27,011,376	3.77	128,748,217
Maine	12,486,977	66.04	76.23	3,893,683	3.21	16,380,660
Maryland	61,627,358	50.00	65.00	33,183,962	1.86	94,811,320
Massachusetts	42,836,231	50.00	65.00	23,065,663	1.86	65,901,894
Michigan	91,585,508	53.58	67.51	44,076,628	2.08	135,662,136
Minnesota	28,395,980	52.14	66.50	14,304,742	1.99	42,700,722
Mississippi	56,017,103	77.09	83.96	10,701,695	5.23	66,718,798
Missouri	51,673,123	60.68	72.48	19,619,817	2.63	71,292,940
Montana	11,740,395	70.56	79.39	3,047,859	3.85	14,788,254
Nebraska	14,862,926	61.17	72.82	5,547,574	2.68	20,410,500
Nevada	30,407,067	50.00	65.00	16,373,036	1.86	46,780,103
New Hampshire	11,458,404	50.00	65.00	6,169,910	1.86	17,628,314
New Jersey	88,417,899	50.00	65.00	47,609,638	1.86	136,027,537
New Mexico	62,972,705	72.61	80.83	14,934,885	4.22	77,907,590
New York	255,626,409	50.00	65.00	137,644,989	1.86	393,271,398

State (or other territory)	Total federal allotments in dollars FY1998[b]	FMAP % FY1998[c]	Enhanced FMAP % FY1998[c]	Estimated state match for maximum federal allocation in dollars FY1998[d]	Estimated federal dollars for each state dollar[d]	Estimated total program expenditures in dollars (federal share +state share FY1998)[d]
North Carolina	79,508,462	63.09	74.16	27,703,596	2.87	107,212,058
North Dakota	5,040,741	70.43	79.30	1,315,805	3.83	6,356,546
Northern Marianas	118,113	50.00	65.00	63,599	1.86	181,712
Ohio	115,734,364	58.14	70.70	47,963,463	2.41	163,697,827
Oklahoma	85,699,061	70.51	79.36	22,288,667	3.84	107,987,728
Oregon	39,121,663	61.46	73.02	14,454,978	2.71	53,576,641
Pennsylvania	117,456,521	53.39	67.37	56,888,916	2.06	174,345,437
Puerto Rico	9,835,550	50.00	65.00	5,296,065	1.86	15,131,615
Rhode Island	10,684,422	53.17	67.22	5,210,285	2.05	15,894,707
South Carolina	63,557,819	70.23	79.16	16,732,503	3.80	80,290,322
South Dakota	8,541,224	67.75	77.43	2,489,674	3.43	11,030,898
Tennessee	66,153,082	63.36	74.35	22,822,146	2.90	88,975,228
Texas	561,331,521	62.28	73.60	201,347,176	2.79	762,678,697
Utah	24,241,159	72.58	80.81	5,756,563	4.21	29,997,722
Vermont	3,535,445	62.18	73.53	1,272,722	2.78	4,808,167
Virginia	68,314,915	51.49	66.04	35,129,838	1.94	103,444,753
Virgin Islands	279,175	50.00	65.00	150,325	1.86	429,500
Washington	46,661,213	52.15	66.51	23,495,475	1.99	70,156,688

State (or other territory)	Total federal allotments in dollars FY1998[b]	FMAP % FY1998[c]	Enhanced FMAP % FY1998[c]	Estimated state match for maximum federal allocation in dollars FY1998[d]	Estimated federal dollars for each state dollar[d]	Estimated total program expenditures in dollars (federal share +state share FY1998)[d]
West Virginia	23,606,744	73.67	81.57	5,333,729	4.43	28,940,473
Wisconsin	40,633,039	58.84	71.19	16,443,852	2.47	57,076,891
Wyoming	7,711,638	63.02	74.11	2,694,027	2.86	10,405,665

Source: CRS analysis of submitted state plans, and *Federal Register*, v. 65, no. 101, May 24, 2000 and *Federal Register*, 45 CFR Parts 92 and 95, May 24, 2000.

[a] Financial information for FY1998 is published in the *Federal Register*, v. 65, no. 101, May 24, 2000. FMAP and Enhanced FMAP figures for FY1998 can be found in the *Federal Register*, v. 62, no. 177, September 12, 1997.

[b] Allotments recorded in this column account for the funding changes described in the *Federal Register*, v. 64, no. 25, February 8, 1999. These changes include a recalculation of state allotments across all years of the program due to a change in the method of counting uninsured children from the Current Population Survey (Section 707 of P.L. 105-277). In particular, children who had access to services through the Indian Health Service (IHS), but no other health insurance coverage are now classified as uninsured which resulted in an increase in the counts of uninsured children in 11 states. The total amount of federal funding available for allotment to the 50 states and the District of Columbia for FY1998 is $4,224,262,500, determined by reducing the FY1998 appropriation ($4.295 billion) by the total amount available for allotment to the territories ($10,737,500) and amounts for the Special Diabetes Grants ($60,000,000) under Sections 4921 and 4922 of BBA. The total amount of federal funds available to the territories is determined by multiplying .25% by the FY1998 authorization ($4.295 billion).

[c] These numbers represent the Federal Medical Assistance Percentage (FMAP) and the Enhanced Federal Medical Assistance Percentage (Enhanced FMAP). They are effective from October 1, 1997 to September 30, 1998 and are published in the *Federal Register*, v. 62, no. 226, November 24, 1997.

[d] The totals in these columns are: (1) estimates of the required state match necessary to claim maximum federal SCHIP allotments; (2) estimates of the ratio of federal dollars spent to each state dollar; and (3) estimates of potential total program expenditures (state share + federal share). Because states have 3 years to draw down a given year's funding and the Enhanced FMAP rates (Enhanced FMAP) are variable from year to year – it is not possible to report a precise dollar amount in these columns.

Table 3. Financial Program Information for States and Territories FY1999[a]

State (or other territory)	Total federal allotments in dollars FY1999[b]	FMAP % FY1999[c]	Enhanced FMAP % FY1999[c]	Required state match for maximum federal allocation in dollars FY1999[d]	Federal dollars for each state dollar FY1999[d]	Potential total program expenditures in dollars (federal share +state share FY1999)[d]
Alabama	85,569,176	69.27	78.49	23,450,032	3.65	109,019,208
Alaska	6,856,760	59.80	71.86	2,685,071	2.55	9,541,831
American Samoa	512,250	50.00	65.00	275,827	1.86	788,077
Arizona	116,246,196	65.50	75.85	37,011,808	3.14	153,258,004
Arkansas	47,681,702	72.96	81.07	11,133,769	4.28	58,815,471
California	850,608,561	51.55	66.09	436,437,227	1.95	1,287,045,788
Colorado	41,593,182	50.59	65.42	21,985,513	1.89	63,578,695
Connecticut	34,793,973	50.00	65.00	18,735,216	1.86	53,529,189
Delaware	8,015,429	50.00	65.00	4,316,000	1.86	12,331,429
District of Columbia	12,018,971	70.00	79.00	3,194,916	3.76	15,213,887
Florida	268,938,576	55.82	69.07	120,432,462	2.23	389,371,038
Georgia	124,071,402	60.47	72.33	47,463,787	2.61	171,535,189
Guam	1,494,063	50.00	65.00	804,495	1.86	2,298,558
Hawaii	8,903,057	50.00	65.00	4,793,954	1.86	13,697,011
Idaho	15,804,712	69.85	78.89	4,229,148	3.74	20,033,860
Illinois	121,949,905	50.00	65.00	65,665,333	1.86	187,615,238
Indiana	70,179,422	61.01	72.71	26,340,207	2.66	96,519,629

State (or other territory)	Total federal allotments in dollars FY1999[b]	FMAP % FY1999[c]	Enhanced FMAP % FY1999[c]	Required state match for maximum federal allocation in dollars FY1999[d]	Federal dollars for each state dollar FY1999[d]	Potential total program expenditures in dollars (federal share +state share FY1999)[d]
Iowa	32,307,161	63.32	74.32	11,163,185	2.89	43,470,346
Kansas	30,511,738	60.05	72.03	11,848,026	2.58	42,359,764
Kentucky	49,696,709	70.53	79.37	12,917,262	3.85	62,613,971
Louisiana	101,256,366	70.37	79.26	26,495,799	3.82	127,752,165
Maine	12,428,004	66.40	76.48	3,822,001	3.25	16,250,005
Maryland	61,336,309	50.00	65.00	33,027,243	1.86	94,363,552
Massachusetts	42,633,928	50.00	65.00	22,956,730	1.86	65,590,658
Michigan	91,152,976	52.72	66.91	45,079,240	2.02	136,232,216
Minnesota	28,261,873	51.50	66.05	14,526,731	1.95	42,788,604
Mississippi	55,752,550	76.78	83.75	10,817,659	5.15	66,570,209
Missouri	51,429,086	60.24	72.17	19,831,945	2.59	71,261,031
Montana	11,684,948	71.73	80.21	2,882,996	4.05	14,567,944
Nebraska	14,792,733	61.46	73.02	5,465,735	2.71	20,258,468
Nevada	30,263,463	50.00	65.00	16,295,711	1.86	46,559,174
New Hampshire	11,404,289	50.00	65.00	6,140,771	1.86	17,545,060
New Jersey	88,000,326	50.00	65.00	47,384,791	1.86	135,385,117
New Mexico	62,675,303	72.98	81.09	14,615,735	4.29	77,291,038
New York	254,419,158	50.00	65.00	136,994,931	1.86	391,414,089

State (or other territory)	Total federal allotments in dollars FY1999[b]	FMAP % FY1999[c]	Enhanced FMAP % FY1999[d]	Required state match for maximum federal allocation in dollars FY1999[d]	Federal dollars for each state dollar FY1999[d]	Potential total program expenditures in dollars (federal share +state share FY1999)[d]
North Carolina	79,132,966	63.07	74.15	27,587,150	2.87	106,720,116
North Dakota	5,016,935	69.94	78.96	1,336,833	3.75	6,353,768
Northern Marianas	469,563	50.00	65.00	252,842	1.86	722,405
Ohio	115,187,783	58.26	70.78	47,552,798	2.42	162,740,581
Oklahoma	85,294,328	70.84	79.59	21,872,814	3.90	107,167,142
Oregon	38,936,902	60.55	72.38	14,858,210	2.62	53,795,112
Pennsylvania	116,901,807	53.77	67.64	55,927,594	2.09	172,829,401
Puerto Rico	39,101,750	50.00	65.00	21,054,788	1.86	60,156,538
Rhode Island	10,633,962	54.05	67.83	5,043,411	2.11	15,677,373
South Carolina	63,257,653	69.85	78.89	16,926,975	3.74	80,184,628
South Dakota	8,500,886	68.16	77.71	2,438,357	3.49	10,939,243
Tennessee	65,840,660	63.09	74.16	22,941,244	2.87	88,781,904
Texas	558,680,510	62.45	73.72	199,160,659	2.81	757,841,169
Utah	24,126,675	71.78	80.25	5,937,718	4.06	30,064,393
Vermont	3,518,748	61.97	73.38	1,276,493	2.76	4,795,241
Virginia	67,992,282	51.60	66.12	34,839,360	1.95	102,831,642
Virgin Islands	1,109,875	50.00	65.00	597,625	1.86	1,707,500
Washington	46,440,845	52.50	66.75	23,133,455	2.01	69,574,300

State (or other territory)	Total federal allotments in dollars FY1999[b]	FMAP % FY1999[c]	Enhanced FMAP % FY1999[c]	Required state match for maximum federal allocation in dollars FY1999[d]	Federal dollars for each state dollar FY1999[d]	Potential total program expenditures in dollars (federal share +state share FY1999)[a]
West Virginia	23,495,256	74.47	82.13	5,112,142	4.60	28,607,398
Wisconsin	40,441,141	58.85	71.20	16,358,214	2.47	56,799,355
Wyoming	7,675,218	64.08	74.86	2,577,544	2.98	10,252,762

Source: CRS analysis of submitted state plans, and *Federal Register*, v. 65, no. 101, May 24, 2000 and *Federal Register*, 45 CFR Parts 92 and 95, May 24, 2000.

[a] Financial information for FY1999 is published in the *Federal Register*, v. 65, no. 101, May 24, 2000. FMAP and Enhanced FMAP figures for FY1999 can be found in the *Federal Register*, v. 62, no. 226, November 24, 1997.

[b] The amount of federal funding available for allotment to the states and the District of Columbia for FY1999 is $4,204,312,500, determined by reducing the FY1999 appropriation ($4,275,000,000) by the total amount available for allotment to the Commonwealths and territories ($10,687,500) and amounts for the Special Diabetes Grants ($60,000,000) under Sections 4921 and 4922 of BBA 97. P.L. 105-277 increased amounts available to the territories by $32,000,000 for FY1999. The total amount of federal funds available to the territories in FY1999 is therefore $42,687,500. Allotments for FY1999 come from *Federal Register*, v. 64, no. 25, February 8, 1999.

[c] These numbers represent the Federal Medical Assistance Percentage (FMAP) and the Enhanced FMAP. They are effective from October 1, 1998 to September 30, 1999 and are presented in the *Federal Register*, v. 62, no. 226, November 24, 1997.

[d] The totals in these columns are: (1) estimates of the required state match necessary to claim maximum federal SCHIP allotments; (2) estimates of the ratio of federal dollars spent to each state dollar; and (3) estimates of potential program expenditures (state share + federal share). Because state have 3 years to draw down a given year's funding and the Enhanced FMAP rates are variable from year to year – it is not possible to report a precise dollar amount in these columns.

Table 4. Financial Program Information for States and Territories FY2000[a]

State (or other territory)	Total federal allotments in dollars FY2000[b]	FMAP % FY2000[c]	Enhanced FMAP % FY2000[c]	Required state match for maximum federal allocation in dollars FY2000[d]	Federal dollars for each state dollar FY2000[d]	Potential total program expenditures in dollars (federal share +state share FY2000)[d]
Alabama	77,012,259	69.57	78.70	20,843,216	3.69	97,855,475
Alaska	7,730,025	59.80	71.86	3,027,037	2.55	10,757,062
American Samoa	538,650	50.00	65.00	290,042	1.86	828,692
Arizona	130,213,077	65.92	76.14	40,804,886	3.19	171,017,963
Arkansas	53,754,360	72.85	80.99	12,617,241	4.26	66,371,601
California	765,547,705	51.67	66.17	391,393,061	1.96	1,156,940,766
Colorado	46,890,416	50.00	65.00	25,248,686	1.86	72,139,102
Connecticut	39,225,273	50.00	65.00	21,121,301	1.86	60,346,574
Delaware	9,036,260	50.00	65.00	4,865,678	1.86	13,901,938
District of Columbia	10,817,074	70.00	79.00	2,875,425	3.76	13,692,499
Florida	242,044,718	56.52	69.57	105,870,645	2.29	47,915,363
Georgia	132,381,325	59.88	71.91	51,711,743	2.56	184,093,068
Guam	1,571,063	50.00	65.00	845,957	1.86	2,417,020
Hawaii	10,036,935	51.01	65.71	5,237,658	1.92	15,274,593
Idaho	17,817,572	70.15	79.1	4,704,956	3.79	22,522,528
Illinois	137,481,231	50.00	65.00	74,028,355	1.86	211,509,586

State (or other territory)	Total federal allotments in dollars FY2000[b]	FMAP % FY2000[c]	Enhanced FMAP % FY2000[c]	Required state match for maximum federal allocation in dollars FY2000[d]	Federal dollars for each state dollar FY2000[d]	Potential total program expenditures in dollars (federal share +state share FY2000)[d]
Indiana	63,161,480	61.74	73.22	23,101,126	2.73	86,262,606
Iowa	32,382,884	63.06	74.14	11,295,136	2.87	43,678,020
Kansas	30,320,974	60.03	72.02	11,779,795	2.57	42,100,769
Kentucky	56,025,995	70.55	79.38	14,553,490	3.85	70,579,485
Louisiana	91,130,730	70.32	79.22	23,904,274	3.81	115,035,004
Maine	13,978,005	66.22	76.36	4,327,397	3.23	18,305,402
Maryland	56,869,698	50.00	65.00	30,622,145	1.86	87,491,843
Massachusetts	48,063,710	50.00	65.00	25,880,459	1.86	73,944,169
Michigan	102,762,059	55.11	68.58	47,080,547	2.18	149,842,606
Minnesota	31,861,256	51.48	66.04	16,384,135	1.94	48,245,391
Mississippi	58,036,226	76.80	83.76	11,252,487	5.16	69,288,713
Missouri	57,979,004	60.51	72.36	22,146,762	2.62	80,125,766
Montana	13,173,122	72.30	80.61	3,168,674	4.16	16,341,796
Nebraska	16,576,269	60.88	72.62	6,249,769	2.65	22,826,038
Nevada	30,526,393	50.00	65.00	16,437,289	1.86	46,963,682
New Hampshire	10,263,860	50.00	65.00	5,526,694	1.86	15,790,554
New Jersey	96,858,666	50.00	65.00	52,154,666	1.86	149,013,332

State (or other territory)	Total federal allotments in dollars FY2000[b]	FMAP % FY2000[c]	Enhanced FMAP % FY2000[c]	Required state match for maximum federal allocation in dollars FY2000[d]	Federal dollars for each state dollar FY2000[d]	Potential total program expenditures in dollars (federal share +state share FY2000)[d]
New Mexico	56,407,772	73.32	81.32	12,957,417	4.35	69,365,189
New York	286,821,535	50.00	65.00	154,442,365	1.86	441,263,900
North Carolina	89,211,202	62.49	73.74	31,769,544	2.81	120,980,746
North Dakota	5,655,883	70.42	79.29	1,477,278	3.83	7,133,161
Northern Marianas	493,763	50.00	65.00	265,872	1.86	759,635
Ohio	129,857,897	58.67	71.07	52,860,405	2.46	182,718,302
Oklahoma	76,764,895	71.09	79.76	19,479,958	3.94	96,244,853
Oregon	43,895,837	59.96	71.97	17,096,017	2.57	60,991,854
Pennsylvania	128,956,235	53.82	67.67	61,610,094	2.09	190,566,329
Puerto Rico	41,116,950	50.00	65.00	22,139,896	1.86	63,256,846
Rhode Island	9,570,566	53.77	67.64	4,578,704	2.09	14,149,270
South Carolina	71,314,037	69.95	78.96	19,002,626	3.75	90,316,663
South Dakota	7,951,348	68.72	78.11	2,228,332	3.57	10,179,680
Tennessee	74,226,011	63.10	74.17	25,849,506	2.87	100,075,517
Texas	502,812,459	61.36	72.95	186,443,825	2.70	689,256,284
Utah	27,199,406	71.55	80.08	6,765,886	4.02	33,965,292
Vermont	3,966,889	62.24	73.57	1,425,104	2.78	5,391,993

State (or other territory)	Total federal allotments in dollars FY2000[b]	FMAP % FY2000[c]	Enhanced FMAP % FY2000[c]	Required state match for maximum federal allocation in dollars FY2000[d]	Federal dollars for each state dollar FY2000[d]	Potential total program expenditures in dollars (federal share +state share FY2000)[d]
Virginia	73,580,365	51.67	66.17	37,618,615	1.96	111,198,980
Virgin Islands	1,167,075	50.00	65.00	628,425	1.86	1,795,500
Washington	52,355,470	51.83	66.28	26,635,885	1.97	78,991,355
West Virginia	21,145,730	74.78	82.35	4,532,145	4.67	25,677,875
Wisconsin	45,591,653	58.78	71.15	18,486,566	2.47	64,078,219
Wyoming	7,068,749	64.04	74.83	2,377,662	2.97	9,446,411

Source: CRS analysis of submitted state plans, and *Federal Register*, v. 65, no. 101, May 24, 2000 and *Federal Register*, 45 CFR Parts 92 and 95, May 24, 2000.

[a] Financial information for FY2000 is published in the *Federal Register*, v. 65, no. 101, May 24, 1999.

[b] The amount of federal funding available for allotment to the states for FY2000 is $4,204,312,500, determined by reducing the FY2000 appropriation ($4,275,000,000) by the total amount available for allotment to the Commonwealths and Territories ($10,687,500) and amounts for the Special Diabetes Grants ($60,000,000) under sections 4921 and 4922 of BBA 97. P.L. 106-113 increased amounts available to the territories by $34,200,000 for FY2000. The total amount of federal funds available to the Commonwealths and territories in FY2000 is therefore $44,887,500. Total appropriations available to states and territories is $4.309 billion. Allotments for FY2000 come from *Federal Register*, v. 65, no. 101, May 24, 2000.

[c] These numbers represent the Federal Medical Assistance Percentage (FMAP) and the Enhanced FMAP. They are effective from October 1, 1999 to September 30, 2000 and are presented in the *Federal Register*, v. 64, no. 7, January 12, 1999.

[d] The totals in these columns are: (1) estimates of the required state match necessary to claim maximum federal SCHIP allotments; (2) estimates of the ratio of federal dollars spent to each state dollar; and (3) estimates of potential total program expenditures (state share + federal share). Because state have three years to draw down a given year's funding and the Enhanced FMAP rates are variable from year to year – it is not possible to report a precise dollar amount in these columns.

INDEX

A

administrative costs, 107-109, 111, 147
adolescents, 93, 109, 112, 142
Agency for Healthcare Research and Quality (AHRQ), 105
Aid to Families with Dependent Children (AFDC), 90, , 91, 95, 107, 111, 118, 140, 155-157
ambulance services, 53, 55, 56
amyotrophic lateral sclerosis (ALS), 50
artificial limbs, 67
available funds, 2, 8, 10, 13, 15, 21-30, 34, 131, 132

B

Balanced Budget Act, 2, 5, 43, 45, 92, 121, 139
Balanced Budget Refinement Act (BBRA), 44, 45, 58-60, 62, 63, 83, 111, 127, 145
beneficiaries, 11, 27, 44, 49-52, 54, 65, 68, 70, 72, 73, 75, 79, 81, 91, 95, 98, 124
Benefits Improvement and Protection Act (BIPA), vii, 5, 8, 11-15, 18, 19, 21-23, 29, 34, 39, 41, 43, 47, 48, 111, 128, 129, 131, 132
Blue Cross/Blue Shield, 123
bonus payments, 58

C

California, 11, 16, 36, 39, 114, 133, 136, 141
cancer, 51, 63
capped allotments, 2
caseloads, 87, 96, 112
cash assistance programs, 91
cash grants, 90, 140
Center on Budget and Policy Priorities (CBPP), 28-30, 94
Centers for Medicare and Medicaid Services (CMS), 2-4, 6, 7, 9, 10, 12, 13, 18-21, 28-30, 34, 38, 41, 124, 125, 130, 132, 135, 137
Certified Registered Nurse, 68
child beneficiaries, 91
clinical diagnostic laboratory, 52, 74
combination approach, 129, 140
Community Hospitals, 54
Community Nursing Organization (CNO), 83
community-based organization(s), 51, 84, 100

Comptroller General, 49, 55, 59, 65, 67-71, 75
congestive heart failure, 50, 79
consultation, 67, 74, 84
consumer price index, 66
consumer, 51, 66
copayment, 49, 52, 130
cost-effectiveness, 52, 88, 89, 104, 157
cost-sharing, viii, 51, 78, 80, 92, 124, 130, 156, 157
coverage determination, 74, 78
critical access hospital(s) (CAH(s)), 52-55
critical access hospitals, 53
Current Population Survey (CPS), 106, 145, 161

D

data collection, 58, 60, 126, 127, 147
deductible(s), 49, 52, 124
delivery systems, 123, 140
dental services, 125
Department Appeals Board (DAB), 73
Department of Health and Human Services (DHHS), 3, 7, 44, 116, 125, 144
diabetes, 48, 49, 50, 126, 144, 145
dialysis, 65
disability, 3, 50, 90, 91, 93, 98, 107, 122, 142
disabled children, 90
disease management, 49, 50
disproportionate share hospital (DSH), 32, 54, 57, 76
durable medical equipment, 66, 74

E

economic growth, 113
education, 76, 88, 108, 126
elderly persons, 84
elderly, 84
end-stage renal disease (ESRD), 65, 78, 81
enrollment statistics, viii, 89
estimated spending, 32, 45
exams, 48
expenditure data, viii, 1, 8, 12, 13, 15, 18-23, 28, 34, 38, 41
extended benefits, 91

F

family income, 32, 91, 102, 103, 116, 119, 124, 129, 141, 155, 156
family incomes, 32, 90, 156
federal allotment, 4, 28, 93, 146
Federal Employees Health Benefits Program (FEHBP), 123
federal funds, vii, 1, 5, 15, 34, 144-147, 161, 165, 169
federal law, 91, 96, 101, 122, 142
federal matching funds, vii, viii, 1, 2, 4, 13, 121, 144, 146, 147
federal matching rate, 88, 93, 107, 108, 147
Federal Medical Assistance Percentage (FMAP), 7, 32, 33, 92, 125, 126, 148, 156, 157, 161, 165, 169
federal poverty level (FPL), 4, 6, 27, 28, 32, 33, 90-94, 101, 116, 117, 121, 122, 124, 130, 133, 135, 141, 142, 145, 146, 155-157
Federal Register, 6, 12, 32, 38, 108, 116, 121, 132, 139, 141, 144, 146, 147, 148, 155, 161, 165, 169
federally qualified health center, 55
fee schedule, 48, 49, 53, 55, 66, 68, 75
fee-for-service, 44, 75, 78
financial standards, 89, 90, 91
financially eligible, 87

food stamp program, 101
foreign-born, 94
funding, vii, 1, 3-10, 14, 25, 27-29, 34, 46, 56, 88, 89, 92, 106, 108, 109, 111, 113, 116, 125, 127, 131, 139, 142, 144, 145, 147-49, 156, 161, 165, 169

G

General Accounting Office (GAO), 7, 44, 53, 64, 68, 69, 71, 76, 85, 94, 96, 99, 128
government, 44, 61, 63, 101, 107, 125, 148
Gross Domestic Product (GDP), 44
gross income standard, 135
group health plan, 3, 81, 92, 122, 123, 140
growth rates, 64

H

Health and Human Services (HHS), 3, 4, 6, 7, 44, 49, 51, 60, 73, 78, 82, 101, 116, 123, 128, 130, 147
health benefit coverage, 147
Health Care Financing Administration (HCFA), 9, 10, 63, 67, 69, 80, 82, 93, 97, 98, 101, 103, 105, 108, 109, 112, 116, 118, 130, 140, 143, 146-149, 155-157
health care fraud, 75
health care providers, 56, 69, 100
health care, 47, 56, 64, 69, 72, 75, 87, 89, 100, 104, 127
Health Insurance Flexibility and Accountability (HIFA), 6, 7, 28-30, 130
health maintenance organization (HMO), 78, 123
health of children, 147
health services, iv, 56, 71, 72, 83, 145

heart disease, 50
home health agencies, vii, 47, 70, 71, 76
home health care, 72
home health services, 56, 71, 72
hospital costs, 57
hospital services, 75, 123
hospitals, vii, 47, 49, 53, 54, 56-58, 60, 62, 63, 68, 72, 75-77, 157
housing, 111

I

immunosuppressive drugs, 50
incentives, 60, 64, 110
income criteria, 90, 91, 96, 140, 155
income standard, 91, 135
increased enrollment, 45
Indirect Medical Education (IME), 57
inflation, 27, 43, 66, 83
inpatient diagnosis, 79
Inspector General, 44, 60, 75
intervention(s), 52, 104, 105

K

knowledge, 96

L

Long-Term Care Hospitals, 58
long-term care, 84

M

managed care, 72, 108, 156
managed health care, 156
market basket index (MBI), 56, 59, 62, 70
market basket, 56, 59, 62, 65, 70, 76
Maternal and Child Health Services Block Grant, 128
media, 68, 100, 106

Medicaid eligibility, viii, 28, 29, 90, 91, 92, 95, 96, 99, 106, 107, 110, 111, 117, 121, 135, 140-142, 155, 156, 157
Medicaid expansions (ME), 10, 93, 98, 119, 129, 130, 140, 142, 143, 147
Medicaid-eligible children, 7, 28, 94, 128
medical assistance payments, 2, 32, 33
medical expenses, 91, 157
medical treatment, 72
Medicare Dependent, 54
Medicare Geographic Classification Review Board (MGCRB), 57
Medicare payments, 54, 57, 59, 60, 70, 72
Medicare+Choice (M+C), vii, 44, 47, 51, 72, 77-83
Medigap, 81
mental health services, 51, 124
mental health, 51, 68, 69, 124
Mexico, 7, 17, 37, 40, 115, 134
model, 28, 80, 105

N

National Association of Insurance Commissioners (NAIC), 49
National Coverage Determination (NCDs), 80
neutrality factor, 79
new technologies, 57, 62
nursing facilities, vii, 44, 47, 60, 63, 82, 85
nursing facility, 44, 56, 60, 76, 82

O

Office of the Actuary (OACT), 29
office visits, 125

Omnibus Budget Reconciliation Act, 141
orthotics, 66, 67
out-of-pocket, 124
outpatient services, 47, 49, 53, 56
outreach expenditures, 108, 147
outreach interventions, 105
outreach strategies, viii, 89, 100, 101, 103, 104, 113
outreach, vii, 11, 73, 85, 88, 89, 99-101, 103-113, 126, 128, 147

P

parents, 7, 28, 94, 95, 110, 113, 130, 157
Part B, 46, 50, 60, 61, 67, 68, 78
pass-through payments, 62
payment provisions, 55
per-visit limit, 56
physicians services, 50, 64, 69
policy change, 27
population densities, 55
population, 55, 77, 90, 94, 99-101, 106, 123, 156, 157
poverty, 4, 6, 90, 93, 94, 116, 121, 135, 141, 142, 145, 155-157
preferred provider, 123
pregnancy, 124
pregnant women, 3, 7, 90, 91, 94, 97, 105, 110, 128, 130, 141, 156
premiums, 49, 51, 61, 78, 124, 135, 156
prescription drugs, 46, 50, 124
preventive services, 104, 125
prices, 56, 71
private health insurance, 6, 130
Program of All-Inclusive Care for the Elderly (PACE), 84
prospective payment system (PPS), 44, 49, 53, 57-59, 61-64, 68, 70-72, 74, 76
prosthetic, 67

psychiatric hospitals, 58
publicly funded, viii, 2

Q

qualifications for community mental health centers, 68
qualified independent contractors (QICs), 73
Qualified Medicare Beneficiaries, 51
qualified practitioner, 67
qualified supplier, 67
qualifying states, 2, 5, 14, 21, 25, 27, 29, 32, 33
quality assurance, 80, 147
quality of care, 97
quality, 51, 71, 80, 83, 97, 118, 147

R

racial and ethnic minorities, 80
reallocated funds, 4, 7, 8, 13-15, 18, 22, 25, 31, 32, 33, 41
rehabilitation facility, 58
rehabilitation hospitals, 58
rural areas, 55, 71, 72
rural health clinic(s), 55, 56
rural hospitals, 54
rural referral centers (RRCs), 54

S

school lunch program, 101
self-administered, 50
separate state programs (SSP), 3, 10, 29, 93, 98, 122, 124, 129, 130, 140, 142
service delivery, 64
skilled nursing facilities (SNFs), vii, 44, 47, 53, 59, 60, 63, 76, 82, 85
skilled nursing facilities, 59
small rural hospital, 54
Small Rural Hospital, 54

Social Health Maintenance Organization (SHMO), 83
Social Security Act, 3, 6, 30, 31, 33, 62, 91, 92, 98, 121, 130, 139, 141, 143
Social Security Administration, 85, 119
sole community hospitals (SCH), 54, 56
Special Supplemental Nutrition Program for Women, Infants and Children (WIC), 101, 111
state laws, 80
statutory objectives, 7
sub-speciality care, 147
Supplemental Security Income (SSI), 90, 95, 98, 107, 118, 156, 157
Survey of Income and Program Participation (SIPP), 106

T

target amount, 54, 58
telehealth services, 55
Temporary Assistance for Needy Families (TANF), 90, 96, 98, 107, 140, 156, 157
tests, 32, 49, 74, 99, 102, 122, 125
thyroid screening, 51
total benefit payments, 147
training, 105, 107
treatment, 52, 54, 78

U

Unemployment Compensation, 101
unemployment, 119
uninsured individuals, 6, 9, 14, 28
uninsured, vii, viii, 1, 3, 4, 6, 9, 14, 28, 32, 89, 92, 94, 101, 105, 106, 113, 123, 125, 127, 130, 140, 141, 142, 145, 146, 156, 157, 161

unspent funds, vii, 2, 4, 5, 6, 8, 11, 14, 18, 22, 23, 24, 25, 26, 27, 29, 31, 34, 38, 128
update mechanism, 65
urban hospitals, 54

V

Veterans Affairs, 79

W

wage index, 57, 58, 60
waiver authority, 84

X

xcoinsurance rate, 49
x-rays, 125